Advance Praise for
Learning from Leaders in Asia
The Lessons of Experience

This extraordinary book is the sequel to *Leadership Experiences in Asia*, Dr. DeKrey's first effort to describe the functioning of leadership in the Asian contexts. There is no-one with better credentials for doing this than DeKrey, an American who has lived and worked in Hong Kong for more than two decades and who has experienced the very best examples of leadership both in the West as well as in Asia. There is no one whose leadership skills cannot be enhanced by the principles and illustrations laid out in this book.

David M. Messick
Morris and Alice Kaplan Professor Emeritus of Ethics and Decision in Management, Kellogg School of Management, Northwestern University

This timely and highly relevant book tackles the critical issues that keep general managers awake at night as they strive to build a sustainable and profitable business in Asia and, in particular, China. The triple challenges of building talent, encouraging breakthrough innovation and ensuring strong governance may be global, but they face added urgency and complexity in Asia given the very high expectations for growth and unique cultural challenges. The blend of theory, strategy and highly practical experience in this book provides invaluable advice for leaders who are determined to build a legacy in Asia.

Ron McEachern
President, PepsiCo Asia

GW00713182

Learning from Leaders in Asia

The Lessons of Experience

Learning from Leaders in Asia

The Lessons of Experience

Steven DeKrey

JOSSEY-BASS
A Wiley Imprint
www.josseybass.com

This edition is published by John Wiley & Sons (Asia) Pte. Ltd., 2 Clementi Loop, #02-01, Singapore 129809 on behalf of Jossey-Bass, A Wiley Imprint.

989 Market Street, San Francisco, CA 94103-1741–www.josseybass.com

Jossey-Bass books and products are available through most bookstores. To contact Jossey-Bass directly call our Customer Care Department within the U.S. at 800-956-7739, outside the U.S. at 317-572-3986, or fax 317-572-4002.

Jossey-Bass also publishes its books in a variety of electronic formats. Some content that appears in print may not be available in electronic books.

Library of Congress Cataloging-in-Publication Data

ISBN: 978-0-470-82509-9

Typeset by Thomson Digital
Printed in Singapore

10 9 8 7 6 5 4 3 2 1

Charles Anderson

In Memoriam

This book, Learning from Leaders in Asia, *is dedicated to Charles Anderson. Charles was the writer of the predecessor to this book,* Leadership Experiences in Asia. *The first book would not have happened without his very capable writing skills, honed by more than 30 years as a journalist. Charles started out doing the same for this book, sitting in on the classes and taking transcripts of the speakers' comments and class discussions. He was about to draft the chapters when he lost his long-running battle with cancer. In his place comes his devoted wife of 20 years, Kathy Griffin, who has picked up his pen and very ably completed the task. Charles is deeply missed by many and for some, lives on in these pages.*

Professor Steven J. DeKrey, Ph.D.
Editor, Learning from Leaders in Asia

> *To laugh often and much;*
> *to win the respect of the intelligent people*
> *and the affection of children;*
> *to earn the appreciation of honest critics*
> *and endure the betrayal of false friends;*
> *to appreciate beauty;*
> *to find the best in others;*
> *to leave the world a bit better*
> *whether by a healthy child,*
> *a garden patch, or a redeemed social condition;*
> *to know that one life has breathed easier*
> *because you lived here.*
> *This is to have succeeded.*
> —Ralph Waldo Emerson

Contents

Acknowledgments

A book of this nature with so many people involved owes its existence to the following. First off, my thanks to the distinguished speakers who came to the classroom to share their experiences. They formed the foundation for the book and even the title. Each of the speakers is a role model for our executive MBA students and all readers of this book. In these times of media attention to leadership foibles these impressive leaders offer a stark contrast and we applaud them and their success. These distinguished leaders are: Mrs. Anson Chan, Mr. Shaopeng Chen, Dr. William Fung, Mr. Ron McEachern, Prof. David Messick, Mr. Stephen Roach, Mr. Jim Thompson, Ms. Marjorie Yang.

Secondly, my deepest thanks to my students, class members of Kellogg-HKUST class 10. These executives took on the challenge of publishing their work and rose to that challenge. They are all leaders in their own right and we thank them for sharing their insights and knowledge as their careers develop. This legacy of our 10th anniversary class is impressive indeed.

This is dedicated to Charles Anderson. Please join me in giving praise to the ground work done by this fine writer. Charles, who helped us write the first book, sat in on each class speaker and helped translate their words into actionable recommendations. Losing Charles mid way through the project as he lost his battle with cancer should have scuttled the work, but in his place his very capable and inspired wife Kathy appeared. It is Kathy whose words we read throughout the piece. She was able to integrate Charles' work with the words and comments from speakers and EMBA students to produce the work you read today. To Kathy, my heartfelt praise and condolences. Charles would be proud.

My role as editor was a management role since most of the writing was done by others. In addition to those above I need to recognize Eva Wong of the EMBA program and her colleagues. Eva handled all the logistics in seeking approvals, corresponding with the many parties and helping me get the project completed. Always with a smile, her competence made this project a pleasure to work on. In addition I need to recognize my personal secretary Anita Lau. Her role was a constant one and without her I would not have been able to do my part on this project or any other. Anita, thanks for this and all that you do and have done for so many years.

Finally, to my beautiful daughters Kimberlee and Katrina and lovely wife Veronica. It is their interest in my work which keeps me motivated and appreciated. To my special ladies, my deepest love and appreciation.

About Our Asian Leaders

In 2007 the Kellogg-HKUST Executive MBA program brought out the book *Leadership Experiences in Asia*, which I co-edited with Professor David Messick and writer Charles Anderson. It was well received and is still selling out there as a composite of leadership case studies and examples of unique ethical dilemmas. The feedback has been good.

Although most of the copies have been selling in Asia, I did pass on a few complimentary copies to my family in Bemidji, Minnesota in the US. My father, Donald H. DeKrey, PhD, to whom the book was dedicated, has read it and has been circulating his copy to his friends. It seems we have found a new market; maybe some will actually purchase copies.

The main comment from my father and friends is that the book offered many interesting insights. The book increased their awareness of cultural differences and gave them insights into global business.

Global business is a concept far removed from Bemidji, my hometown. The closest the 15,000 residents there come to global business is a visit to the local Wal-Mart Super Center. And visit this store they do. Its impact on my hometown is impressive yet alarming.

In addition to expanding the buying power of the local residents, it has also greatly affected the businesses run by many of my friends.

The price competition, impressive inventory, and buying processes adopted by Wal-Mart, a global giant in both retail and procurement, are more than many of my friends' businesses can compete with.

In response, they are adopting strategies of service and quality products. But the price competition is almost insurmountable. So, in the end, we can say that global business, especially Asian activity through which Wal-Mart sources many of its products, does have an impact—even in Bemidji.

In this second book, *Learning from Leaders in Asia*, we take the role of adviser to global leaders in Asia on specific agenda items. The first step was to define the agenda and for this, we drew on the insights of a group rich in experience in Asian business: our tenth Kellogg-HKUST EMBA students. Let me explain why their views matter.

The Kellogg-HKUST EMBA program is among the top three EMBA programs in the world, according to the *Financial Times*, and we have held that ranking since 2005. The program is a joint venture between the Kellogg School at Northwestern University and the Business School at the Hong Kong University of Science and Technology. Faculty members from each institution share their expertise, resulting in a natural blend of Eastern and Western concepts. At the end, graduates earn a joint MBA degree co-signed by each institution.

The executive students, our authors for this project, are drawn from across Asia, and have on average 14 years of work experience. They are in leadership positions, with many senior titles represented and an average annual compensation of $250,000. These are serious students of management and significant leaders across Asia. There is no dominant national culture represented, because there are more than 14 nationalities in this class. It is a truly global sample of leaders. (You can see a full list of their names and titles at the end of this chapter.)

To help set the agenda for this book, I devised a survey asking them what issues they thought Asian leaders should focus on. Eight areas were considered worthy of concern, which form the contents of this book:

- talent recruitment and retention;
- globalization;
- China strategies;
- stability, both economic and social;

- innovations;
- corporate governance;
- marketing strategies;
- social responsibility.

Each topic was assigned randomly to small groups of our EMBA students, who were asked to write a book chapter for an Asian readership interested in global business focused in the region. We also invited distinguished speakers, established leaders in their fields, to share their insights and provide another perspective. Their input can be found throughout the book, along with a short biography of each speaker in appendix 1, but let me give you a brief introduction:

- Anson Chan, former Chief Secretary for Administration, Hong Kong Government;
- William Fung, Group Managing Director, Li & Fung Ltd.;
- Ron McEachern, former President, PepsiCo International for Asia;
- Stephen Roach, Chairman, Morgan Stanley Asia Pacific;
- Chen Shaopeng, President, Lenovo Emerging Market Group; Senior Vice President, Lenovo Group;
- James Thompson, Chairman, Crown Worldwide Holdings Ltd.;
- Marjorie Yang, Chairman, Esquel Group.

I also share insights in my capacity as Senior Associate Dean, Adjunct Professor of Management, and Founding Director of the Kellogg-HKUST EMBA Program.

The chapters produced by the EMBA students became their final project, and include their own research, their personal experiences working in Asia and the insights from the distinguished speakers. The result is *Learning from Leaders in Asia*, which I trust you will find enlightening about the challenges facing leaders in Asia today.

Widening the view: alumni survey

An interesting context for this book is a survey we conducted of all alumni and current students of the Kellogg-HKUST EMBA Program. Of the eight issues identified by Class 10, we wanted to find out how they were ranked among a wider group of business executives in Asia.

Our alumni are well placed across Asia and have the unique qualifications of all being prepared professionally with masters degrees in business administration through the Kellogg-HKUST EMBA Program and having years of leadership experience in Asia.

Our students and alumni total 521. Of those, we asked only those working across at least two countries in Asia to respond: 214 alumni responded, representing 41 percent of the total population. For any type of survey research such a response rate is worth celebrating. Thanks to all our alumni out there.

Key to our questioning was the relative importance of leadership challenges they face in their work in Asia. They were asked to rank the eight challenges identified by Class 10 alumni in order of importance. Here are the results:

Leadership Challenges Ranked by Alumni
Talent: recruitment and retention, 31 percent of respondents placed
    this at the top;
China strategies, 18 percent;
Globalization, 14 percent;
Economic and political stability, 12 percent;
Innovations, 12 percent;
Corporate governance, 7 percent;
Marketing strategies, 6 percent;
Corporate social responsibility, 1 percent.

Across Asia, the need for talent is huge. One alumnus offered an anecdote that even when you find great talent, the growth rate of opportunities grows faster than the skills of the people. So keeping up, even with very good people, can be problematic.

This is a problem that continues today, even though these surveys were conducted before the financial meltdown in the latter half of 2008. Companies need strong and capable leadership. It's not simply an issue of numbers, but of finding the right people. The training we provide in the Kellogg-HKUST EMBA helps to fill that gap by developing leadership talent in Asia.

Since talent issues are widespread, we invited our respondents to tell us where they find the best people for leadership positions in their companies. The results, in table 1.1, show that internal development is a key solution.

Table 1.1: Sourcing global leadership in Asia

Source	Ranked no. 1	Ranked among the top three
Company development programs	31%	52%
Returnees	23%	66%
Local recruiters	20%	52%
American expatriates	11%	41%
Hong Kong natives	9%	41%
European expatriates	5%	29%
Singapore natives	1%	18%

While it is clearly a critical requirement to develop leadership talent inside companies, the pipeline is not full. That means external recruiting is necessary. Our respondents find returnees (native Asians who have moved away and returned), and candidates identified by local recruiting, are important in filling the gap. Expats from various places have also been brought in, but may not be the best source of leadership talent in Asia.

There was no shortage of talent in our KH10 class of executives, who all held senior management positions at the time of writing and came from a diverse range of industries, such as IT, banking, tourism, consumer products, property development, management consulting, pharmaceuticals, broadcasting, and telecommunications, as you can see from the list that follows. Over to them, and our distinguished speakers.

About our authors

The War for Talent

Johnson Chen, General Manager for a manufacturing firm
Gaby Koren, Vice President of Sales for an IT firm
Vincent Lam, General Manager for a manufacturing firm
Jose Rico Adega, Director of Business Promotion in China for a government body

Brian Sung, Director of Business Operations for a power generation investment company

James Tai, Senior Director of an electronics firm

Cindy Tay, Head of Go-to-Market in a telecommunications firm

Wendy Yuen, Senior Manager in investment services for a bank

Globalization and Asian Business

Clarence Chung, Executive Director and Group COO for a conglomerate

Stephane Guesnier, Central China Area Director for an international logistics firm

Gurinder Singh, Vice President for a construction and infrastructure firm

Dariusz Sus, Director of E-Business Operations in Poland for an outsourcing firm

Casey Wang, Vice President of Finance in a bank

Michael Yong-Haron, Executive Director of a private bank

China and the Go West Policy

Jerry Chang, Managing Director for a management consultancy and executive search

Joshua Chang, Principal and CEO of a logistics firm

Terence Kam, Regional Finance Director of an entertainment and fitness company

Elan Lam, Chief Operating Officer of a security firm

Alex Liu, Partner in a legal firm

Patrick Liu, Founding Partner of an Internet and telecom company

Timothy Miller, Chief of Staff and Managing Director of Travel and Consumer for a business services firm

Achieving Stability in a Volatile World

Chris Bailey, Partner in a legal consultancy

Pow Chin, Center Support Manager for an advertising firm

Wendy Gan, Executive Director of a property company

Chris Pagan, Vice President of institutional client group of a bank

Bernard Woo, Associate Director of a market research firm

Joseph Yeung, Founder/Director/CFO of an Internet firm

Peter Zhang, Greater China Business Leader for Talent and Organization Consulting Analytics for a consulting firm

Innovate and Lead

David Buck, Chairman of the Board of an IT and BPO outsourcing firm

Michael Chan, Taiwan COO of a bank

Sylvia Chen, Senior Marketing Manager for a computer firm

Angela Dong, Finance Controller—China and Hong Kong for a trading firm

William Hsu, Vice President of Advertising Sales for a media outlet

Casandy Ng, Director of a retailing firm

Peter Tsang, Head of Betting Services for a jockey club

The Changing Landscape of Corporate Governance

Jeff Albright, CEO of a powered-equipment provider

Catherine Chan, General Manager of Investor Relations for an Internet firm

Sang Soon Hyun, Chief Executive of an investment bank

Derek Ku, Senior Manager of Customer Relations and Loyalty Program for a tourism enterprise

Linda Tang, Finance VP and Controller in Asia-Pacific for an IT company

James Tobin, Region Commercial Manager in Asia-Pacific for an energy company

Building Brands Across Asia

David Brickler, Executive Director of Technology and Security Risk Services in a commodities trading firm

Dilip Chathanath, Chief Operating Officer of an IT services firm

Patrick Chen, Senior Manager of a manufacturing firm

Tomer Feingold, Director of a finance company

Dong-Soo Lee, Marketing Director in a pharmaceuticals company

Jessica Zhang, Consulting Practice Leader in Greater China for a
    consultancy

Corporate Social Responsibility: Enlightened Self-Interest

Johann Albano, Manager, Asia Business Development in the consu-
    mer/food industry
Bobby Chen, Director/Assistant President in a property business
Sheila Cheng, Research and Business Manager—Asia in a medical
    device company
Steve Lai, Regional Director for a utility
Flora Li, General Manager of Industry Training and Resources in a
    media company
Jeff Sayed, Head of Operational Risk for a bank
Gabriel Shriki, Business Development Manager for a communications
    company

Chapter 1

The War for Talent

In the modern-day business environment, competition in the marketplace has intensified from the basis of product and price, to the core of a business organization—what many human resources (HR) professionals describe as "The War For Talent."

A business organization is by definition a group of people assembled to accomplish common objectives or goals, such as maximizing the profits of investors, catering to new lifestyles and trends, or performing a particular service for customers or society for a fee. The key element no doubt is *people*. People set out the structure, business model, and governing modus operandi of an organization. People also bring various functions of the organization together and produce synergy. Particularly in the service sector, employees are an organization's most important asset.

It is therefore logical to conclude that any top-performing company, whether a multinational or local small and midsize enterprise (SME), must have an effective approach and framework for attracting and selecting talent. The result of the "War for Talent" is that businesses must be competitive in attracting and selecting the necessary people, and must ferret out the rare individuals who can eventually take up leadership positions and drive the company forward.

What we present here is a step-by-step framework for talent management and leadership development. We will refer to a few study surveys to illustrate the latest broad trends, and use the example of the Lafarge Cement Company Chinese joint venture to show successful HR in practice. In all of this, we hope to provide some unique and helpful insights into the practice of talent management in Asia.

What is "talent"?

We all want talent, whether it is as individuals looking to make our mark on the world or as companies wanting to hire a body of capable workers. But just what is "talent"? A dictionary definition offers a few clues: *1: A special natural ability or aptitude, 2: a capacity for achievement or success, 3: A talented person, 4: A group of persons with special ability, 5: A power of mind or body considered as given to a person for use and improvement* (*www.dictionary.com*). But in truth talent is something more complex than that. It is partly innate, partly learned, and it can be subject to other dynamic forces. For example, having talent without accompanying moral standards is the equivalent of a walking time bomb because that talent could be deployed, in the worst case, in a way that is harmful to society and the business community.

Attributes of talent

Intelligence is essential to talent and it helps to be aware of its different forms. For instance, IQ (intelligence quotient) measures cognitive capacities, while EQ (emotional quotient) measures our ability to recognize our own feelings and those of others, motivate ourselves and manage emotions well internally and in our relationships.[1] The abilities ascribed to emotional intelligence are distinct from, but complementary to, academic intelligence, that is, IQ.

Talent, we would argue, is similarly differentiated by hard and soft qualities. The former (hard) is usually related to learned sciences, such as mathematics, engineering, and physics, while the latter (soft) deals with the softer expressive skills that are harder to learn and relate more to personality, such as painting, music, emotional control, or sociability. The good news is leadership, management, and technical skills can be developed and learned through experience and education, though social skills are more related to personality and a person's mindset.

In business, the standard approach in developing talent has been to acquire more technical abilities, but current trends show a drift toward endowing our leaders with softer skills, such as being able to adapt to a diversified environment.

Ethical values and talent

Talent is also distinguished by ethical values. Talented managers may be great at management and analytical skills, but this doesn't necessarily relate to their moral values. For instance, Enron Chairman Kenneth Lay and CEO Jeffrey Skilling are both sophisticated and brilliant businesspeople, yet their unethical business practices overshadowed their talents. Is it desirable to have talent without business ethics, like these Enron executives or those at WorldCom (Nanda 2003)?[2] The growing emphasis on business ethics for today's leaders means that personal integrity has become a major consideration in selecting corporate leaders.

Ethics is the steering wheel, while talent is the vehicle being driven. It really depends on how the leader implements his or her talents and in what direction. With the introduction of the Sarbanes–Oxley Act in 2002 to govern corporate accounting and auditing compliance, the integrity of corporate leaders becomes a significant factor when selecting talent. Finding the right people who also have the correct personal values to fit the company's culture and mission has become very important.

Attracting talent in Asia

Attracting talent is difficult all over the world, but the situation is even more complicated when the battlefield turns to Asia. This broad geographical region is rich with many distinct histories, cultures, languages, value systems, and people. Furthermore, countries at different stages of economic development are juxtaposed, and external failure issues such as spillover, exploitation, and wage differentials are all a common part of daily operational conflicts that organizations need to resolve. Bribery and reliance on personal relationships to move business forward are prevalent in Asia, particularly in newly developing countries.

Political economy also comes into play, such as the various rules and factors that restrain the mobility of talent across borders. What we can observe today in rapidly growing Asia as a whole is a unique interaction of all these socioeconomic factors, sometimes co-existing perfectly, sometimes clashing with each other. In summary, Asia is nothing like the Western analytical framework that traditional theories have been based on.

Although it is rather risky to make generalized claims about attracting talent in Asia as a whole, there are some commonalities that can be derived from the complex situations that abound. These can help to provide business enterprises in the region with insights into and practical ideas for finding talent.

An interesting place to start is with prospective talents themselves. What qualities in a company attract MBA graduates? This is an interesting question because MBA training provides graduates with sophisticated analytical approaches and tools that can be useful to corporations worldwide.

A survey of MBA graduates from leading international schools was conducted by public relations consulting firm Hill & Knowlton in 2007. It found that "company reputation" was the most important factor for choosing which company to join. Furthermore, the respondents identified the five top drivers defining company reputation— things like the quality of management, the quality of products and services, employee talent, financial performance and investment value, and innovation (see table 1.1). In particular, Asian MBA

Table 1.1: Hill & Knowlton survey of MBA graduates (2007)

Factors in Company Reputation	Percentage that Rate this Extremely or Very Important
Quality of management	89%
Quality of products and services	88%
Employee talent	83%
Financial performance and investment value	71%
Innovation	68%
Global reach	58%
Social responsibility (significant in Asia)	58%

students ranked corporate social responsibility (CSR) highly, significantly more so than their counterparts in North America and Europe.[3]

Further insights into what defines "company reputation" can be drawn from another survey on "The Best Employer in Asia," carried out by international leading personnel consulting firm Hewitt & Associates and the *Wall Street Journal Asia*.[4] It surveyed employees of 750 companies across the region and came up with the rankings in table 1.2. The top-ranked companies had in common a humane and friendly working environment and an effective personnel management policy. These employers were credited with promoting self-motivation and they had the full trust and high regard of their employees. They also enjoyed an edge over their competitors, with a comparatively lower turnover rate of an average 10 percent per year.

When comparing the two studies, it is no surprise to find that the factors that make these companies tops among employees are also the ones that MBA graduates consider desirable. Management quality, product and service quality, and employee talent can only be produced and developed in a working environment that encourages self-motivation and drive, and provides a clear track and goal for its employees. The Hewitt survey further indicated that respecting the organization and the leadership in the organization is a universal element affecting employee loyalty across Asian cultures.

Table 1.2: Hewitt & Associates, best employer in Asia survey (2007)

Ranking	Company Name	Market	Origin
1	FASL Semiconductor (AMD-Fujitsu JV)	Suzhou, China	USA/Japan
2	Three On The Bund Group	Shanghai, China	Singapore
3	Ritz Carlton Hotel Hong Kong	Hong Kong	USA
4	Shangri-La Hotel Kerry Center Beijing	Beijing, China	Hong Kong
5	Four Seasons Hotel Singapore	Singapore	USA
6	Sales Force	Australia/NZ	Australia
7	Marriott Hotel India	India	USA
8	SK Telecom	Korea	Korea
9	Four Seasons Hotel Shanghai	Shanghai, China	USA
10	Southern Lee Kum Kee Mfg. Ltd.	Guangzhou, China	Hong Kong

A surprising finding in the Hewitt survey is the performance of local and joint venture businesses over multinationals. Traditionally, multinational corporations (MNCs) had the advantages of an established reputation, established corporate structure, and career development path to attract talents. They easily attract highly talented individuals with multilingual capabilities and employees who have a strong desire or expectation to work in a multicultural environment and are open to the notion of job assignments. However, in the Hewitt survey, Asian firms did very well. FASL Semiconductor, a US–Japan manufacturing joint venture operation in Suzhou, came out on top. Three on the Bund, a Singaporean restaurant/real estate group, came second, and the Guangzhou manufacturing unit of Lee Kum Kee, a Hong Kong-based food processing firm, came tenth. Hotels also scored well—despite their overseas parent company heritage and management system, they are often operated independently and locally with relatively few staff.

We can therefore conclude that a solid corporate reputation built on ethics, integrity, and quality management, which encourages respect and promotes self-motivation in employees, is the best assurance for drawing in new talent and retaining it. It is wise and useful for businesses to consider investing in and working on these traits, regardless of the company size, industry or markets, whether local or multinational.

Talent retention and training in China

Companies all around Asia are facing challenges on the talent front, perhaps nowhere more so than in China. Not only can it be a trial to hire new staff, it can sometimes be even more difficult to retain them.

With 1.3 billion citizens, one might think China had an endless pool of available workers. This is true for several types of professions and work requirements. However, when it comes to skilled managers who need to face problem-solving situations and aggressive growth demands, China is at a huge deficit. Even though universities are increasing student quotas and accepting more students, their graduates have little actual experience in the field, and often lack enough of the soft skills required to perform in today's competitive environments.

Moreover, MNCs also want their Chinese employees to have sufficient English-language skills so that they can communicate within the company and globally, plus experience dealing with a global corporation in a multicultural setup. As more and more companies enter into China, the competition among MNCs over the few available skilled managers who can fit that profile is increasing, and salaries are skyrocketing.

This situation has led to the current situation of sourcing three distinct groups of skilled staff: expats, locals, and "hybrids."

Sources of talent

Expats, or expatriates, are transferred in to provide highly skilled, highly paid management and to oversee strategy, business development, government relations, and business units. They also maintain the company culture and open connections with headquarters. Employing expats is usually an expensive proposition. Not only are they paid high salaries, but their packages often include housing and schooling allowances, car and driver, and more. The extras can depend on the city they are assigned to—in some cases there may be additional bonuses and "compensation" for agreeing to live and work in certain locations.

There are several challenges in employing expats. One common concern is that these individuals often don't understand Chinese culture, and are distant and less involved with the local employees, so they fail to create a unified company culture. Expats are a temporary solution; organizations tend to want them to train and prepare local managers to take over management responsibilities. A Deloitte & Touche consultant suggests that when appointing expats, "key selection points are cultural awareness (more important than 'sensitivity'), curiosity and a strong family and marriage." Language skills, though rare, can often make the difference.

Local hiring, on the other hand, is very straightforward. Most employees in the Chinese operations of corporations will be locals, with salaries within the market range. Challenges arise, though, when skills are in short supply, for example, in areas outside the main cities. Companies may then have to rethink their compensation packages (see the Lafarge Cement case that follows).

"*Hybrid*" workers are becoming more popular among MNCs in China, and encompass a variety of subcategories of employees. One prominent group is returnees, who are Chinese born, have lived overseas, and have returned to China. They offer a combination of China–West language and cultural knowledge, experience in international environments, and ease in communicating with the outside world. Another group of interest is foreigners who have lived in China for years. One of their most attractive characteristics is that they are not employed under a full expat package, so it is expected that their commitment and tenure will be longer. Retention is a key consideration for hybrids, though—they have the highest rate of turnover because the market is very hungry for employees with these types of experiences and skills. In a sense, hybrids could be seen as a natural replacement for some of the jobs eventually freed up by expats. This is a good reason to focus on retaining them.

Retention

In a 2006 survey of companies by Mercer Human Resource Consulting Company, 87 percent of companies said turnover was a key organizational problem, and about 60 percent thought the problem was getting worse.[5] More and more companies treat the problem strategically because they recognize that turnover affects business growth (see figure 1.1). Retention of employees has been a top objective for HR practices in companies operating in China.

Figure 1.1: Employee turnover: impact on business

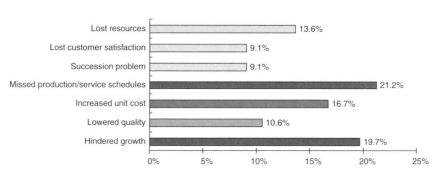

Source: Mercer.

Figure 1.2: Top 10 factors in retaining talent

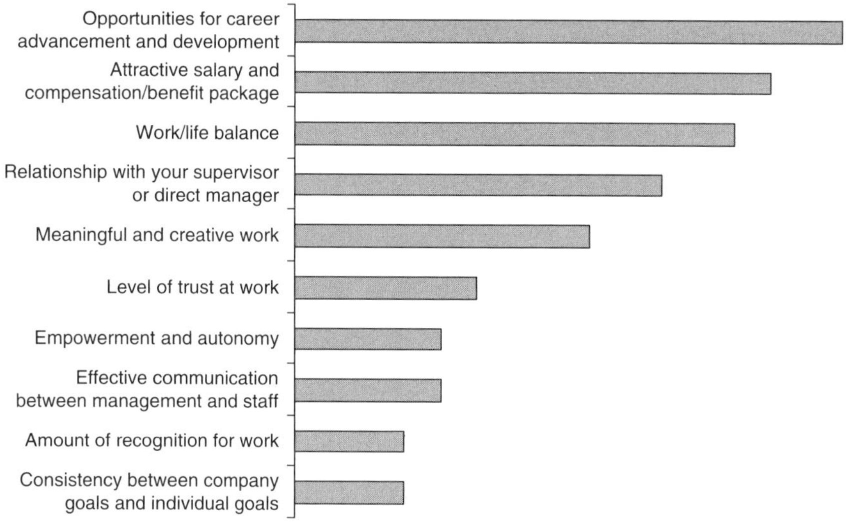

Source: Mercer.

A basic requirement for retaining talent in China is to understand what motivates employees. Although salaries keep increasing due to the competition over skilled employees, it would be wrong to say salaries alone are the number one motivator. Mercer found that other factors also hold sway when it comes to retention. Opportunities for career advancement and development topped the list (see figure 1.2), ahead of cash and compensation. This is strongly linked to the Chinese sense of family tradition, respect, and caring for the younger generation, according to other research. Companies that create a positive working environment and show employees they have a future there enjoy lower turnover rates.

Case Study: Lafarge Cement

The various human resources challenges faced by China today can be illustrated through the case of Lafarge Cement. Lafarge is the world's number one cement producer. It operates in more than 80 countries and has its home base in France, having been in existence

(*continued*)

(*continued*)

since the mid-1800s. Safety and people development are at the heart of its managerial responsibilities and it does not take them lightly. Almost 50 percent of bonuses for senior managers worldwide are tied to these two components.

LAFARGE IN CHINA

Lafarge entered China in 1994. It started small then expanded its operations, inaugurating its new Dujiangyan cement plant in 2002, the first greenfield cement plant for the Lafarge Group in China. This would be one of many investments in the country and a small sample of what was to come.

In 2005, Lafarge entered into a joint venture with Shui On Construction & Materials Ltd., a subsidiary of Hong Kong's Shui On Group. Lafarge owns 55 percent of the entity. A significant milestone was achieved in May 2007, when the China Central Government approved its acquisition of Sichuan Shuangma Investment Group for RMB305 million. This made the company the largest cement producer in southern China and a wholly owned foreign enterprise.

Lafarge's cement production in China is expected to be greater than in any other country it operates in by 2012. It needs people to fuel that expansion. At the end of 2006, it had almost 12,000 employees in China and by early 2008 nearly 18,000, rivaling the workforce of its North American operations. This rapid growth, while very welcome, presented challenging human resource issues. However, Lafarge has a management system that enabled it to deal with the potential problems.

LAFARGE'S HR APPROACH

Lafarge has a global talent pool and a core of expatriate workers who are transferred around the world. The first CEO of Lafarge Shui On was Cyrille Ragoucy, formerly the president of Lafarge Canada. One of the challenges faced by Lafarge and all other international companies is language. The official language for Lafarge's business meetings worldwide is English. Hard to believe for a premier French company, but true. The approach in China has been to partner senior managers with Mandarin-speaking,

(*continued*)

native Chinese counterparts. Many of the positions being posted for senior management have a requirement today for fluency in Mandarin, and it is no longer common for senior leaders to be non-Chinese. It's also interesting to note that while much is said of the need for *guanxi* and relationships in China, this has not been the approach of the French as they traveled the world, cementing their position as the world's leader in construction materials.

Lafarge's localization efforts also include drafting local Chinese HiPos (high potentials) into the talent pool. They are given assignments in different parts of the world to build experience, then rotated back to China in leadership roles. This is a strategy that has worked fairly well for the company in many countries. No doubt, as these local HiPos mature, they will eventually join the senior ranks of executive leadership. China represents a huge part of the Lafarge Group's future, and having proper representation of that future on the board of directors is seen as a necessity.

Leadership is not the only focus for localization, though. Local employees are also replacing expats in other strategic areas, including production, maintenance, and environmental and safety standards. There are complications in this. Lafarge needs skilled mechanical, electrical, and industrial engineers and, while these are abundant in China compared to other places, such as North America, they are not always easy positions to fill. Challenges arise when staff or recruits, many of them younger individuals, realize that they must relocate to smaller communities. Cement plants produce pollution (breaking big rocks into smaller and smaller rocks is hard to do in an environmentally neutral way), so many facilities are found outside the big cities, or increasingly forced to locate there. Luring the younger generation away from city bright lights and shopping is not the easiest thing to do, especially in a competitive environment. Lafarge, though, has been able to develop a compensation package that attracts the right skill set from this demographic. Progress is being made and HiPos within this group are being moved around the world to give them additional experience.

Lafarge's efforts to educate employees about the "Lafarge Culture" and encourage rotation of employees around the world, thus opening up career paths, has helped it to retain staff in China and elsewhere. The case shows that a strong corporate culture can transcend national, cultural, and language barriers to develop a common bond among employees.

Leadership development in Asia

The ultimate goal of HR management is to identify and develop potential leaders who can steer the company onward. Leaving natural talent undeveloped is like having uncut rough diamonds—there is no shine. To bring out the luster of talent, liberalized systems need to be established to encourage talent development and expression. HR managers should also bear in mind that leadership development is not only about training individuals to lead a team, it's also about polishing interpersonal relations in the company to tighten the "chemical bonding" among team members. An HR system that promotes team play, integrity, trust, initiative, humanity, and diversity has become essential in today's business environment.

Talent can be developed by wisely using the human resources that a company already has at its disposal. Good internal management systems and a structure that offers employees opportunities to advance in their careers can help a company succeed financially. An often quoted example of this is Southwest Airlines. Southwest employs very few MBAs and most of its employees have minimal qualifications, but it is still a successful and efficient business compared to its competitors.[6] Another example is Procter & Gamble, which also does not bring in stars (for example, top MBAs from Harvard or Stanford), yet is one of the most successful consumer-product companies in the world.[7]

Our research into talent retention and our own experiences have shown that there are a few things companies can do to develop leadership capabilities among their staff:

- *Invest in proper training.* Soft skill training is recommended alongside technical and professional training. This shows that the company is serious about investing in its employees and equipping them to perform their duties well. Moreover, this training also gives important insight about individual employees, their values, and other significant skills that might not be apparent when they carry out their daily job. Employees should have opportunities to explore and develop their strengths and weaknesses.
- *Provide career paths and development.* When an employee sees a future in the company and a clear career path, chances are that he or she will not only be motivated to stay, but will be motivated to

excel. Career paths should be clearly communicated to employees by the company; it should not be assumed the initiative will come from the employee. There should be an objective, comprehensive personal development plan based on individual assessment results (for example, the PDP—Professional Dynametric Program—and the Hogan Development Survey) and past performance that aligns with the company's or group's strategic targets.

- *Rotate staff.* Employee rotation can have significant long-term benefits. Employees who are interested in exposure to other cultures and opportunities will be very positive about this option and the new experiences will excite and motivate them.
- *Promote cultural understanding.* A lot of companies use the word "global" when describing their operation, but there needs to be something to back that up. Companies should teach employees about cross-cultural considerations and behaviors, to increase tolerance and avoid conflicts. This is especially true for international assignments, allowing expats to understand the intrinsic cultural characteristics of their host country clearly.

A good first step is to establish a plan with clear goals for talented individuals that is supported with innovative learning or training programs. Moreover, individuals should be encouraged to practice leadership skills and make continuous improvement based on fair assessments to reinforce their successful development as leaders in the company.

Summary: completing the framework

Talent retention will likely be an issue in China and Asia for some time to come, but it is not an insurmountable problem. Companies should bear in mind that their integrity and reputation play a role in attracting and retaining the kind of people who, as their hard and soft skills mature, can help drive an organization to further success.

Companies should also consider that providing career and personal development programs could help them hold on to capable and promising employees. The surveys cited in this chapter showed that this was a top consideration among employees in China, which we take as a positive sign. It shows that talented recruits are no longer drawn by cash and compensation alone, or even by whether a company is a multinational. Although it means HR management has to take a more sophisticated approach, it also shows that any business, regardless of size, can attract talent if it offers the right combination of career-leadership development opportunities, job satisfaction, achievement, and compensation.

So companies in Asia take note: the best universal policy for attracting and retaining talented people is to build up a reputable, ethical business organization. These people could ultimately become leaders in the firm or, at the very least, be quite likely to have high individual satisfaction, which can help improve productivity and give the company a critical edge. As HR managers have declared, this is not just a fight for talent, *this is a war.*

STEVE DEKREY, Associate Dean and Director of MBA/EMBA/MSc Programs, Hong Kong University of Science and Technology

"It's not just numbers. We need a new brand of leader."

The sophistication demanded of talent in this part of the world magnifies the war for talent. It's not just the numbers, it's being able to manage in a complicated environment. You have different cultures, languages, countries, the East–West dynamic—all these complications that managers have to be able to negotiate. The people who can handle all of this are few and far between. So the dearth of leadership is magnified by that.

This is why the leaders in our program see talent as issue number one. It's become so serious that it limits the growth of companies and they can't capitalize on opportunities.

What we're trying to do here at the School of Business is address the high-level demands in this part of the world. It's not just numbers. We need a new brand of leader.

I started out in my work in Asia trying to identify the Asian leader. I've given that up, it doesn't exist. We need global leaders. Identifying the Asian leader isn't useful.

No doubt I can find differences between Chinese and American business leaders, but it isn't useful. The typical leaders from these

(*continued*)

places can't take companies to global levels. We need visionaries who are responsive, open-minded, multicultural, driven by curiosity.

These kind of people are very hard to produce. The best place to find them is among returnees who have done their education in the West. That's why we're here, we're providing a Western-style education in Asia.

So what skills does a global leader need to have? When you talk about leadership there are three general components: knowledge, skills (what you've done in practice), and outlook (personality, interpersonal skills, leadership orientation).

Our program provides all three—some form of experience, formal and informal knowledge, interpersonal development, and so on. And we add global into the mix through multicultural leadership interactions, teaching across cultures—these things you can't learn in many places. You need contact with people from elsewhere, live sharing in the classroom to bring the global perspectives to life. There is a shortage of opportunities for learning in such an environment. So we help leaders to develop their skills.

The success of global leadership also depends on the attitude of leaders. I've seen surveys done of executives to see who can adapt best to an expat international life. Get this—one of the key questions that relates highest with successful overseas assignments is whether you enjoy trying different types of foods. It's one of the best predictors because it shows openness to differences, a willingness to embrace and try new things.

Sometimes you can get managers who are very successful in their countries but they are dogmatic and don't have the open mind you need to succeed in a global environment.

Global leaders need to be open and intellectually curious. They are listeners, not talkers. How else do you lead a multinational team, without listening? Or deal with the unique political environment of China? Or figure out what headquarters wants? Team leadership, an open mind and an open door are critical in balancing all of these demands.

Notes

1 Daniel Goleman, *Working with Emotional Intelligence* (New York: Bantam Publishing, 1999).

2 Ashish Nanda, "Broken Trust: Role of Professionals in the Enron Debacle," *Harvard Business Review*, February 2003.

3 Hill & Knowlton, "Eighth Corporate Reputation Watch," 2007.

4 Hewitt & Associates, "Best Employer in Asia Survey," April 2007, www.best employerasia.com.

5 Mercer Human Resource Consulting, "Snapshot Survey of 'Top Ten Factors to Retain Talent,'" 2006.

6 Malcolm Gladwell, "The Talent Myth," *The New Yorker*, July 2002.

7 Ibid.

Chapter 2

Globalization and Asian Business

We live today in a world that has no boundaries. A world where a product labeled "Made in China" may have parts from Italy, India, and Vietnam, but is just assembled in China. A world where a US customer calls the service hotline of his local telecommunications provider, but is connected to a call center in the Philippines. Thomas L. Friedman described this phenomenon of globalization in his book *The World is Flat*. The "flatteners" are creating a whole new

> global, web-enabled platform for multiple forms of collaboration. This platform enables individuals, groups, companies, and universities anywhere in the world to collaborate—for the purposes of innovation, production, education, research, entertainment, and, alas, war-making—like no creative platform ever before. This platform now operates without regards to geography, distance, time, and, in the near future, even language. Going forward, this platform is going to be at the center of everything.[1]

It has already changed the way we do business. Innovations in communications and technology are bringing together people, resources, information, services, and capital flow at a faster rate than ever.

Globalization changes countries and the lives of those who live in them. Since the early 1990s, China has transformed itself into the "world's factory," using its abundant supply of relatively cheap labor to manufacture affordable goods for major world economies such as the US, Japan, and the European bloc. India, too, has capitalized on its human resources, in particular skillful software engineers, to become a major provider of outsourced computer programming. However, that is not the whole story. Globalization has stirred up new challenges, even as it has helped countries to exploit their competitive advantages for economic growth. In this chapter, we examine the impacts of globalization on the world's economies and financial markets, the new competition regime it has brought about, and the talent issues it has given rise to. These issues all have lessons for economies and individual companies trying to bridge East and West.

Can Asia buffer itself in a global economic downturn?

The most important question for Asia in a globalized world is whether it can stand on its own. Is it robust enough to weather slowdowns in its main markets in the US and Europe, a global recession and stalled growth, as witnessed in 2008? After a decade of Asian growth, spurred by the rise of China and India, some pundits believe it can. They see a third economic bloc that is large enough to absorb any downturn in the US or European markets. As Asian leaders consider their responses to events, though, they need to ask themselves what assumptions they should make about global contagion and Asia's decoupling from the rest of the world.

The good news about globalization is that global growth is much more diversified across the developed world and emerging markets than a decade ago. China and India alone contribute about 41 percent of the world's economic growth. Economic developments over the past decade have created a three-horse race—emerging economies as a bloc, Europe and the US (see table 2.1).

The million-dollar question, though, is how well Asia can ride out a US-led slowdown. The economic slowdown in 2008 has showed that problems in one region cannot go unnoticed in others. As a large supplier of goods and services to North America and Europe, Asia has been inevitably affected by events beyond its borders. Its increasing

Table 2.1: World real GDP annual growth

(% change year ago)	2004	2005	2006	2007	2008f	2009f	2010f
World	3.9	3.4	4.0	3.8	3.1	3.5	3.7
US	3.6	3.1	2.9	2.2	1.2	1.9	3.0
Canada	3.1	3.1	2.8	2.6	2.0	2.4	2.5
UK	3.3	1.8	2.9	3.1	1.5	2.0	2.6
Eastern Europe	7.2	6.2	7.0	6.7	3.0	5.7	5.2
Eurozone	1.8	1.6	2.9	2.7	1.7	2.0	2.3
Australia	3.9	2.8	2.8	3.9	3.4	3.2	3.0
China	10.1	10.4	11.1	11.5	9.3	8.5	8.8
India	8.3	9.2	9.4	8.8	8.5	8.5	8.4
Japan	2.7	1.9	2.4	2.1	1.6	1.9	1.6
Asia-Pacific excluding Japan	7.4	7.2	7.7	8.0	7.0	6.7	7.1
Latin America and Caribbean	5.7	4.2	5.1	5.0	4.8	4.4	4.4
Latin America (weighted average)	6.3	4.7	5.3	5.3	4.2	3.9	4.1

f = forecast
Source: Beth Ann Bovino, senior economist at Standard & Poor's.

specialization and dependence on globalization for its growth have deepened its ties with the rest of the world.

The figures show just how much Asian economies rely on exports. Exports make up 37 percent of GDP in China, 37 percent in Korea, 59 percent in Taiwan, and 72 percent in ASEAN countries as a whole. This reliance was on an upward trend up to 2008. In China, exports as a share of GDP had almost doubled since the early 1980s when they were just less than 20 percent, while the GDP share for consumption plunged from 67 percent to 36 percent. However, Asia's exports to the US have actually declined over the past decade, in some countries significantly, as figure 2.1 from Credit Suisse shows. This suggests Asia has been achieving a partial decoupling from the US in terms of export dependency.

Figure 2.1: Asia's partial decoupling from US slowdown

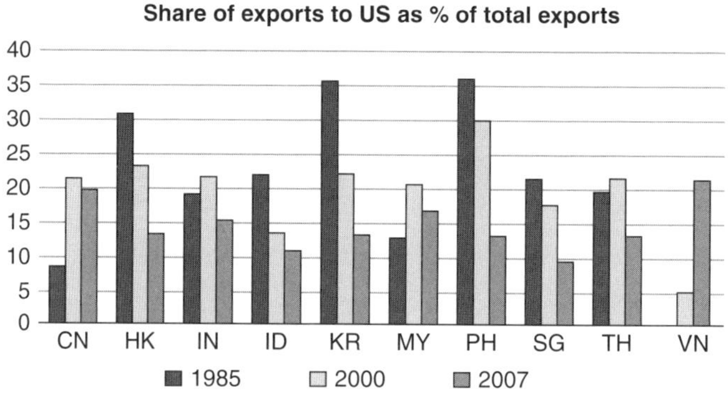

Share of exports to US as % of total exports

Source: Datastream, IMF, Credit Suisse.

Can China, and Asia, save the world in a downturn?

Asia's lower reliance on US exports raises the question whether growth in this region can pick up the slack in a global economic downturn. Since 2000, the economic growth cycles between emerging countries and developed economies have shown an interesting divergence, as figure 2.2 shows. On the down cycle, emerging countries experience shallower contractions than developed economies, while on the up cycle they rebound at a much faster pace. Although Asia is interconnected with the rest of the world, and is not immune to

Figure 2.2: Strong economic growth in emerging markets

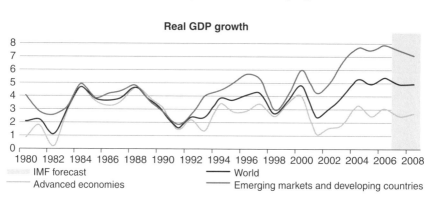

Real GDP growth

Source: Datastream, Credit Suisse.

a slowdown, especially when it happens in developed countries, it has evolved over the past decade into an economic bloc. It is no longer just a supplier to the Western world—it is trading more within the region and developing domestic consumer and infrastructure sectors. Suffice it to say that when the West catches a cold, Asia sneezes. But it now seeks relief with Chinese herbal medicine and Indian Ayurvedic and Asian remedies, and it has a good shot at recovering faster than the developed world.

But can China and Asia extend their recoveries to save the rest of the world in an economic downturn? The short answer is probably not. India and China have been dubbed "little monkeys" compared to the US consumer market. It's easy to see why. As of 2007, US consumers spent $9.5 trillion a year, compared to a combined $1.5 trillion spent by China and India. No matter how hungry the new consumers of Asia are, they still cannot rescue the world through their consumption.

China's imports are small, about 6 percent of the world's total. Where it makes an impact on the rest of the world is through its demand for natural resources—things like metals, coal, agricultural produce, and machinery equipment. When exports cool down and private capital expenditure slows, then China and others like it in Asia will need to rely on government infrastructure spending to maintain their growth momentum.

How Asian governments can respond in a down cycle

What goes up inevitably comes down. When it comes to economic downturns, governments can soften the landing, but they need to tread carefully in the minefield between direct intervention and letting markets sort things out. Here are some things they can do.

Develop their domestic economies. Asia's growth has depended on exports in general, and exports to the US, Europe, and Japan in particular. This is risky because it makes the region susceptible to external shocks. To counter this, Asian governments and leaders need to speed the development of their domestic markets through their own national brands. We have seen this happen quite successfully in Korea with Samsung, Cheil, Lotto Shopping, Hyundai, Kia, and so on. China is catching up through powerful national brands including Lenovo, China Mobile, China Telecom, Mengniu, Great Wall, Want

Figure 2.3: Fixed asset investment

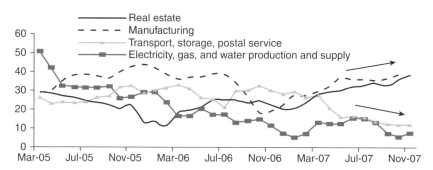

Source: Credit Suisse Private Banking Research Department, "Asia fixed assets investment trends," Credit Suisse Investment Outlook, December 2007.

Want, and Tingyi. Other countries in Asia need to do the same, at a faster pace and with a sense of urgency.

Invest in infrastructure spending. After a period of robust investment in infrastructure, at an average rate of 20 percent of their budgets, Asian governments started to slow down investment toward the end of 2007, at least in some areas, as figure 2.3 from Credit Suisse research shows. This could not have come at a worse time. Export growth plunged months later and domestic consumption has not been large enough to lift the entire economy. The situation calls for *more* government spending and expenditure to keep the economy going, not less. Investments should be made in underinvested areas such as transportation, electricity, energy, and water infrastructure.

Learn from the 1997 Asian Financial Crisis. In 1997, the Thai baht collapsed, triggering the Asian Financial Crisis. Thailand's experiences then, and again 10 years later when the country faced another currency manipulation, offer lessons to others. The 1997 collapse followed an overvaluation of the currency and a decision to drop the peg to the US dollar. In the more recent case, the baht was undervalued. It started to strengthen and the Thai Central Bank imposed capital restrictions on all foreign investors. The effect was dramatic. There was a 16 percent selloff of the Thai stock market the next day, leading Thai policy makers to reverse most of the measures quickly.

For investors doing business in Asia, the big question is what lessons other Asian policy makers are learning from this debacle. The Thai experience can be read two ways. On the one hand, it shows that policy makers should not mess with the markets, and any intervention in foreign exchange markets would be counterproductive and therefore pointless. But on the other hand, it may reinforce policy makers' belief that any rise in their currency must be managed gradually by the government.[2]

Given that the Asian Financial Crisis has left deep scars on the current generation of policy makers, they are more likely to stick firmly to the latter option. Expect them to keep a close eye on their currencies to prevent "overshooting" (which forces them into extreme measures), and to take action well ahead of time.[3] Central banks are not afraid to use extreme measures to prevent their currencies from rising by any more than they feel is reasonable. As far as Asian currencies are concerned, policy makers would rather keep their currencies undervalued than risk them being overvalued. The Asian Financial Crisis showed how difficult it is to intervene in such a situation.[4]

Concern has been raised that keeping Asian currencies artificially weak may risk more serious longer-term problems with inflation. However, many Asian central banks are taking their cue from China as far as revaluation is concerned. China is an obvious target for trade bashing and has been under Western pressure to massively revalue its currency. The Chinese yuan already discounts a revaluation of +9 percent in the non-deliverable forward market. As Dong Tao, Chief Economist of Credit Suisse APAC, has said, the level of the yuan is a political decision and any revaluation will be done in an orderly and gradual fashion. With the vast foreign currency reserves China has amassed, the Chinese Central Bank has plenty of ammunition with which to keep the yuan low by buying US Treasuries and even acquiring US companies. This trend looks certain to continue.

Never again the IMF, but how about an Asian Stability Fund? There is still much debate about the IMF's role in exacerbating the Asian Financial Crisis. One crucial blunder was the dissonance between its supposed (and original objective) of global stability and its then newfound objective of capital market liberalization. The IMF's harsh fiscal austerity measures, coupled with the imposition of high interest rates, created a collapse of aggregate demand in Asian economies when economic revival was needed. In addition, the IMF's approach of treating all Asian economies the same way helped to spread the contagion like wildfire.[5]

A few Asian leaders have instead proposed the creation of an Asian Stability Fund. Its two objectives would be to provide funds to restore aggregate demand in countries facing economic recession, and to be a regional surveillance watchdog that puts pressure on Asian countries to maintain their economic strength, focusing on inflation, unemployment, and growth.[6] The wealth is there to carry off such a fund. Asian countries have learned the lessons of the Asian Financial Crisis and built currency reserves so large that they have spawned sovereign wealth funds. While the equity acquisitions made through these funds can enrich an individual country's influence, it is high time to set aside some of their reserves and pull together to form an Asian Stability Fund. Asian leaders need to think ahead and prepare for down cycles, so that Asia as a whole can weather such crises better and stronger.

Asian business in the global economy: case studies for staying competitive

In this world with no boundaries, it can be hard to pin down the dominant players. For several decades, American and European MNCs were seen entering Asian markets to acquire companies with potential, and capturing markets with their brands and products. But lately, the trend has reversed. Asian companies are acquiring foreign companies. They are also building their own brands and entering foreign markets. For instance, Samsung has successfully transformed into a premier household name in major Western markets. Another successful example is Lenovo. After acquiring IBM's PC business, it decided not to use the IBM brand on its PCs, and switched to the Lenovo brand earlier than required. Lenovo has continued to innovate and lead the PC sector, winning more technology innovation awards after the acquisition. Samsung and Lenovo are by no means Asian exceptions. Many Asian companies have successfully transitioned into the global marketplace, where the keys to continuing success are innovation, flexible adoption of local and best practices, and talent management. In the following case studies, we look at how two companies applied this winning formula.

Case Study: Melco International: Reinventing Itself and the Gaming Market in Macau

Melco, short for the Macau Electricity and Lighting Company, has been listed on the Hong Kong Stock Exchange for more than 80 years. In 2001, new leadership took over the company after the expiration of its electricity franchise, and it set off in a new direction. The company moved into the leisure and entertainment business, with Macau's gaming market its primary focus. Before 2002, gaming in Macau had been a monopoly under Dr. Stanley Ho, but the Macau government policy changed and Melco saw an opportunity. The government has issued six new gaming licenses—one of them to Melco and its partner, Australian conglomerate, Publishing and Broadcasting Limited (PBL).

REINVENTING THE GAMING MARKET

The company arrived at a time of transition in Macau's gaming market, and set out to shake things up. Before 2004, the market was dominated by table games, especially high-roller/VIP tables. Slot machines were not at all popular, and casino operators put minimum attention into promoting them. By contrast, in Las Vegas, slot machine wins comprise more than 50 percent of total gaming wins. After studying the world market and considering local circumstances, Melco decided on a slot machine-only venue in Macau, a move that was new to all markets—most slot machines are placed in a casino together with table games. Melco introduced the Mocha Slot Hall brand (www.mochaclubs.com) in 2003, with a dedicated team to market the product and to provide the right environment, as well as high-quality services for customers. It was a great success, and effectively created a new market segment in Macau that caters to local Macanese and returning customers from Hong Kong and surrounding Chinese cities. The result: the slot machine market in Macau has grown and Melco has continued to take a major market share of it.

EAST MEETS WEST

After the market was liberalized in 2002, Melco recognized that to be competitive it needed to bring in international gaming expertise.

(continued)

(*continued*)

However, it also believes that you cannot just replicate success from overseas without adjusting to the local environment and local situations. With that in mind, it selected PBL as its partner in the Macau market, and it has proved to be a good fit. PBL has deep experience serving Asian high rollers back in its casinos in Melbourne. Melco went on to build the first six-star hotel in Macau, the Crown Macau, targeting VIP customers, whereas other casino licensees such as Las Vegas Sands and Wynn are building Vegas-type properties catering for both mass and VIP markets. Crown Macau opened in May 2007 with about 220 rooms and 210 gaming tables, against the 3,000 suites, 800 gaming tables, and 3,400 slot machines in the Venetian Macau, and 300-plus gaming tables and 500-plus slot machines in the Wynn Macau. Crown has maintained an air of exclusivity, for VIPs only, and in February 2008 achieved an 18 percent share of the total Macau gaming market with less than 10 percent of the total gaming tables. That made it the world number one in terms of gaming revenue generated in a single property.

Melco also successfully listed its Macau gaming assets on the NASDAQ stock exchange in December 2006, and raised more than $1.25 billion through its IPO, tapping international funds for its expansion in Macau.

Case Study: Li & Fung: Agents of Globalization

Strikingly, some Asian corporations have become globally competitive by defining and deploying their own business model. Take Li & Fung, for instance: not only did it pioneer the use of the Internet to bridge frontiers, it also brilliantly developed its own global strategy to support business expansion.

Li & Fung, which has its headquarters in Hong Kong, is one of the largest "managers" of supply chains for other companies in the world. The company integrates and orchestrates the flow of information and goods among thousands of factories in emerging markets and final customers around the world. It is actually pushing globalization a step further by connecting suppliers from developing countries with top-brand companies from the US and Western

(*continued*)

Europe. In doing so, Li & Fung heavily relies on applied IT technologies, and is quite often considered to be an IT company. There are two core concepts in Li & Fung's successful strategy.

BORDERLESS MANUFACTURING AND GLOBALIZATION OF MANUFACTURING

This means going to the best place for components or processes and eventually finding a place for final assembly. That's a "Made by China" product as opposed to a "Made in China" product. This is the epitome of globalization. It doesn't matter where it's made; what matters are the price and quality of a given component.

OFFSHORING AND OUTSOURCING MODEL

As have other outsourcing companies, Li & Fung has waited patiently for its clients to change their mindset toward offshoring and outsourcing. The improving quality and flexibility of offshore manufacturers and increasing cost competition mean more and more Li & Fung clients are comfortable offshoring their production. Once that decision is made, Li & Fung works hard to propose a competitive source, thus taking over the client's operations completely, as shown in the table.

	In-house	Outsourced
Onshore	Principal's natural space	Importer's natural space
		L&F onshore strategy
Offshore	Principal's own buying office	L&F's natural space

Li & Fung has a truly global approach, well beyond its regional arena. It builds on the strengths and advantages of various countries and regions, acting as a bridge between customer markets (US, Western Europe, and Japan) and production countries (developing countries).

The company has defined its own model of manufacturing. Owning 100 percent of the production chain obligates you to take on all of the production, and creates unnecessary rigidity in the manufacturing structure. So Li & Fung owns at maximum 60 percent, and enjoys a greater deal of flexibility. This helped it to

(continued)

(*continued*)

address a recent trend toward work in short production runs. Li & Fung's model also departs from the very clustered Detroit Model, where several tiers of suppliers are all located around a key manufacturer, which spreads resources and regionalizes markets.

Loosely coupled networks and orchestration skills are key to making the new supply chain cooperative and collaborative, as opposed to the traditional buy-and-sell adversarial relationships. Management of the supply chain at Li & Fung is clearly sequenced and crosses borders, and takes the following path:

1. consumer needs
2. product design (in the countries of consumers)
3. product development (in the production countries)
4. practical side
5. vendor compliance
6. raw materials sourcing
7. factory sourcing
8. manufacturing control
9. shipping control
10. forwarder consolidation
11. customs clearance
12. local freight forwarders
13. wholesale
14. retail
15. consumer

This global organization has ensured competitiveness even when there are international trade hurdles and economic difficulties. A case in point is the US preference for encouraging trade with partners such as Mexico to raise employment and slow down the emigration of labor. Li & Fung understood this dynamic and established very sizable structures there.

Another issue the company has dealt with successfully is the quality of toys. Li & Fung is strong in monitoring the manufacturing process. After recent quality issues with Chinese manufactured toys, it managed to convince its customers that its offer was right in terms of total service cost to buyers.

Yet another issue has been cost escalation in China. Li & Fung can shift its resources from export commodities to consumer products and production to lower-cost countries in a matter of months.

(*continued*)

> To support globalization and entrepreneurship, Li & Fung is organized into 150 small units, with each given a lot of freedom. It lives globalization every day, making sure the flow of goods and information never stops.

The examples of Melco and Li & Fung provide insights into how company leaders can develop and position their businesses. There are two key points here. First, they need to critically review their company's value proposition on a constant basis, with reference to the market situation and their competition. That means being willing to reinvent themselves constantly. Second, company leaders need to "look globally and act locally." Understanding the local situation and its constraints is important, and companies should adapt their activities appropriately. Company leaders also need to be flexible in responding to new circumstances.

Managing global talent: two views from the inside

Any discussion about globalization is incomplete without considering the challenge of how to manage people across countries and cultures. Here, two management consultants share their experiences of managing talent in globalized environments in Hong Kong and China.

Crossing Cultures in Management Consultancy

By Casey Wang, who at the time of writing was Senior Consultant, Global Business Services, IBM China/Hong Kong Ltd.

In a service-driven business such as management consulting, talent management is critical to the success of delivering client advisory services in all major industries and helping companies to build long-term, profitable growth.

I work in the strategy and change practice at one of the top five management consulting companies in the world. It was once known as a technology company, but now has a presence as a consulting organization in 160 countries. We offer a spectrum of services

(continued)

(*continued*)

including strategy and change, customer relationship management, supply chain management, financial management, human capital management, application innovation, application management services, and business transformation outsourcing. With the shift to a service and customer-centric business model, it has been critical to attract talented people who can support the model and build capability in client delivery services.

The talent pool at a global consulting company is built up at the country, regional, and global levels to provide people who have the kind of expertise that can be transformed to meet client demand anywhere. In the case of Hong Kong and China, the hiring needs are varied due to local business requirements and environmental, political, and social movements, and forecasted projects in the pipeline.

TALENT PROFILE

Two kinds of consultants are in demand in management consulting in China and Hong Kong: graduates, through campus recruitment, who are academically high achievers with strong business analytical skills, and experienced hires with deep industry knowledge and "been there, done that" experience. They are trained up to become top professionals who can learn, act quickly, handle stress well, be flexible and mobile, and be inspired long-term.

My company has been ranked one of the top global companies to work for in China. We look for graduates from top and reputable universities, such as Beijing University and Tsinghua University, who have solid educational backgrounds, as well as experienced hires from industries such as telecommunications, government, products, and financial services who have knowledge and experience about local business operations and Western companies based in China.

Historically, Hong Kong has been service driven because of its position as a center for international finance and distribution services. Clients require experienced consultants with a Western mindset and local industry knowledge. In recent years, we have seen a rise in interest in Hong Kong Chinese who have business degrees from overseas universities and exposure to Western working culture.

(*continued*)

TALENT MANAGEMENT APPROACH

The market is changing fast in locations like China and Hong Kong. As a global company, it is important for us to stay aware of the needs of globalization and to assess the ability of countries and consultants to develop their human capital based on different measures of competitiveness. My company understands the urgency of keeping its consultants updated with knowledge, and readily equips them with training and learning opportunities. They can fly into a location for central training or conduct online training courses through a knowledge portal for self-study purposes. There are often discussion forums held for all locations to brainstorm specific topics.

The company offers a competitive retention package, including attractive compensation and retention programs. It aims to build all-round experts with a selected special focus. Other important initiatives include the development of internal training and external recruitment programs, exploratory and pilot job rotation, the re-engineering of performance evaluation, and career planning mechanisms. The company has, for example, established an individual key performance indicator to increase the transparency and effectiveness of performance evaluation, set up mentoring schemes, and reframed its recruitment program to attract talent (for example, campus recruiting, career websites, career fairs).

Talented people in a global management consulting company are increasingly required to work out of their location and learn how other business operations and corporate cultures work. This is a common requirement within the company and a great example of the impact of globalization on the consulting industry.

A recent experience showed how cultural integration and cooperation is being applied in a foreign owned business in China. A project was signed with the Hong Kong practice that required Chinese human capital management (HCM) knowledge—something the Hong Kong office could not provide. Because the China office has a strong HCM team, we had Shanghai HCM consultants work with Hong Kong team members to deliver the project. They helped the client standardize the company's payroll structure and streamlined the HR processes. The Shanghai consultants applied HCM methodology and, together with customized best industry practice to suit the client environment, they gained the client's trust, which led to a successful implementation. Hong Kong

(continued)

(*continued*)

team members were able to learn HCM skills from the Shanghai team, and Shanghai consultants learned how to manage foreign clients and communication skills.

Another example was a Hong Kong client that needed a benchmark of how its organization compared with other similar organizations globally. We used the global talent search engine in the company to get an expert from the US to walk the client through how other organizations faced their current market challenges, while also sharing some of the lessons learned by other global organizations. Injecting the right expert greatly increases credibility and demonstrates our deep understanding of the industry as a whole. On other occasions, we have had China experts come to Hong Kong to advise our clients in Hong Kong and vice versa.

In management consulting, the unavoidable effects of globalization have been the need for appropriate talent management to handle cross-cultural work, the deployment of standardized and structured methodology and strategy, and the ability to equip clients with world-class solutions to tackle the challenges of the global marketplace.

Key Challenges

Compensation in the management consulting industry is competitive, but on average it is lower than for in-house consulting roles in other industries. Once consultants work for several years in a specific industry they can build subject matter knowledge and become valuable to that industry. Accordingly, consulting is always at risk of losing talent.

However, that is not the only concern. When consultants work for a foreign client or outside their location, although they are experts in the business, they may lack understanding of the local culture, have limited experience with foreign client relationship management, and come up against language barriers. When doing business in other cultures, many consultants underestimate cultural sensitivities and lack people knowledge, creating conflicts with the project goal and alienating the people working on it.

Standardization might not apply to all locations due to geographical, cultural, political, and social differences. A methodology that works in one place either might not work or might not even be required in another. Consultants need to have an open mind and be

(*continued*)

ready to change and modify methodology when approaching clients in different regions.

Best industry practice can be developed when consultants gain experience working in different regions and with different clients. However, some consultants who have great industry and hands-on experience in a specific country may not have the same success in another country. Their expected best practice might not be the best practice for some clients.

In sum, there are three key things a management consulting company can do to develop a strong talent pool:

- Delegate authority (work on more exposure, variety).
- Empower (value-adding, personal growth) and compensate.
- Blend teams with local and foreign talent.

You want talent to come to you and you want it to feel your company is the best place to work. People managers should offer exposure and interesting project opportunities for consultants, delegate them to the next work level, and create opportunities for them to prove themselves. Working with talent from the region and in global teams, consultants can practice their language skills and develop themselves as cultural integrators.

More reward programs and incentives should be established to recognize high performers, while leadership teams should communicate personally with high performers and show appreciation for their contributions. This can stimulate their career advancement and create a value-adding mentality within the company.

Capgemini: Making the World Flat in Guangzhou

By Dariusz Sus, who at the time of writing was Global Head of BPO Product Development, Capgemini US

Until recently, I was in charge of Capgemini's business process outsourcing (BPO) in Greater China. We had set up a delivery center in Guangzhou as a natural low cost, near-shore location for Hong Kong. Within a couple of years, we became one of the most

(*continued*)

(*continued*)

diverse service organizations in China, servicing clients from four continents. Less than 10 percent of our servicing was for Chinese operations. The rest covered the Asia-Pacific region and 25 other countries—in their native languages. The work is as far from data processing as one might expect. It includes all accounting functions as well as handling complex billing issues and management reporting. How could this happen in a country where shortages of talent had been the leaders' number one concern?

It certainly wasn't an easy task. Like other multinationals, Capgemini develops relationships with local universities and colleges and offers internships. But these activities did not bring any advantage over the competition. We needed something different.

My biggest surprise after being transferred from Europe was the diversity within Asian countries. Looking at Asia, most Europeans think of it as Europe, but a bit larger and more populous. When I started to learn more about Asian history, I found that national borders did not necessarily follow nationalities, and the official language was sometimes not even spoken by 50 percent of the population. Also, the mobility of the workforce within China and between Asian countries seemed very high. With that in mind, my company started looking at where particular languages and skills could be found, and how we could transfer these people to Guangzhou.

One organization we turned to was the Catholic Church, whose hundreds of thousands of missionaries traverse Asia in the evangelical cause. The Church meticulously gathers data on all citizens, including languages spoken and beliefs, as a matter of course. We also contacted a few universities in Hong Kong to understand why, for example, Dutch is still taught in Jakarta at all law faculties, what more than 20,000 Korean speakers were doing in Manila, and how different the Portuguese spoken in East Timor was to that used in Brazil. All this information transformed our approach. From then on, we were literally cherry-picking candidates from different places in Asia-Pacific, avoiding expensive and ineffective recruitment campaigns in Guangzhou.

We also combined the HR team with operations to analyze work outsourced from clients. That way, we could break it down into

(*continued*)

pieces that require a foreign language and ones that do not. There were parts of the job that needed specialized knowledge and parts that did not. In the end, it might happen that what one accountant was doing on the client side was done by four Capgemini employees. This helped make recruitment very skill focused and effective. We also had fewer problems with retaining such employees, because they were less attractive on the market.

Globalization of the workforce certainly forces HR managers to be more innovative and courageous. The ethnic and cultural diversity of Asia can be weighed against a shortage of talent. Although combining different cultures required a whole lot of work, the end result was a strong team that can compete in the world's service markets.

Conclusion

In obtaining products for different markets, managing diverse workforces all over the world, and predicting global financial markets, Asian business leaders have quickly learned what it takes to compete in a rapidly globalizing world. Lenovo's story of its move from local PC maker to a truly global technology company has been an inspiration to many. "Having a global market is an incentive to innovate more," Columbia University professor and economist Joseph Stiglitz has said. Lenovo certainly has such an incentive. Li & Fung, too, has excelled at orchestrating the global supply chain.

Globalization creates enormous opportunities as well as threats to Asian companies. It demands thinking beyond one's country or region—a different kind of entrepreneurship where business leaders are more forward thinking and always prepared. A local market may suddenly be eliminated by multinationals with greater experience and time to recoup early losses. Over the next 25 years, it is quite likely that globalization will spread and the world will "shrink" even further, deepening trade, cultural, and financial links. Asian leaders need to master skills outside their local curriculum. A global perspective is not just a value-added trait, it has become a critical factor for success.

WILLIAM FUNG, Group Managing Director, Li & Fung Ltd.

"This is the industrial structure of the future."

When it comes to the globalization of manufacturing, "offshoring" and "outsourcing" are sometimes used interchangeably. They are actually very different. You can be General Motors, and you can offshore by building a car in China, but you still own the plant. If you buy the cars from "Chery Auto" in China, that's outsourcing. There's a big difference.

Li & Fung's success is based on the fact we are riding a mega trend—the trend toward offshoring labor-intensive manufacturing of our kind of consumer goods. It's an unstoppable trend. For the past 40 years, it's just been happening.

There's a whole concept behind borderless manufacturing, through the evolution of different kinds of manufacturing.

Take the making of shoes. In America, it started in Massachusetts, went down to the south of the country and then over the border into Mexico. Younger people in America, the developed economies in Europe and Japan, are no longer willing to go into this kind of factory operation. This is something that underlines and supports our business. And I don't see that kind of trend changing in any way.

In terms of outsourcing, nothing is sacred these days. Absolutely nothing. People look at what they need in their company, and anything that is not absolutely strategic is a candidate for outsourcing.

It wasn't too many years ago that nobody thought about outsourcing IT or accounting. But right now nothing is a sacred cow. People say, if somebody else can do this better than I can, if these are not the key things that we do that distinguish us and our business, then I want to outsource it if somebody else can do it better.

A lot of our principals, the retailers who work with us, the brands who work with us, start off by being in-house and onshore. They start off by being in America, they do their buying in-house and they do it in America.

Li & Fung's natural space is offshore and in the outsourcing area. If companies wanted to continue this sourcing or buying of garments, they would have their own buying office. If they wanted to stay onshore, they would work with importers. If they don't want to come overseas, and they just want to work with New York or London, they would work with importers. So there's a natural space for everybody.

(continued)

But if they want to outsource and want to go offshore, they have to organize independent buying operations at a natural source. It depends what a company wants to do. The chances are there's a combination.

Basically, it works this way. Some companies use their own buying office, and also buy through importers. This was the way globalization started. They buy from importers, and then realize it is better to buy directly themselves and bypass this level. They either come to us, or start their own office.

This is the progression in terms of globalization and the way it has moved. We don't look at manufacturing countries. We look at manufacturing in different markets and we go to the best place for our components or our processes, wherever they may be.

In the old days, this could be "made in Hong Kong" or "made in China." Nowadays, what tends to happen is a product such as an outdoor jacket may be designed in America, the lining could be from a company called Taiwan Taffeta, one of the biggest lining companies in the world, and the shell fabric could be some kind of microfiber or nano fabric from Korea. The zipper could be YKK from Japan. The filler might be from China and the whole thing might be assembled in China.

Instead of a product being made in China, it is somehow made by China. It's a combination of different products.

It's not just us. Take one particular brand of laptop. The chances are the monitor is from Taiwan, the memory from Penang, it's assembled in China with the most valuable part—Intel—inside.

People thought about making everything in-house at a time when transport costs were really high. Then came the vertically integrated Detroit Model with all the expertise under one roof and the suppliers or subcontractors clustered around.

The idea now is to have a dispersed manufacturing model where you go to the best of breed or the best place in the world to manufacture. Basically, you have dispersed manufacturing and you bring it back together with supply chains.

Right now, thanks to the development of logistics, lowering of costs associated with them, and the development of IT, you can actually do that. That's what we do; we orchestrate these loosely coupled networks. We think that's the industrial structure of the future.

STEPHEN ROACH, Chairman, Morgan Stanley Asia Pacific

"Don't take globalization for granted."

Globalization is probably the most widely used construct and concept in this increasingly integrated world economy. But I think it is also the least understood. My profession, the economics profession, has done an absolutely terrible job of articulating the stresses and strains of globalization. We must come to grips with it if we are going to steer the course of a globalized world economy.

We tend to lapse into this mindless mantra and talk about global issues as always being "win–win" situations. I can't tell you how many conferences I have been to in China where it says, "win–win globalization, win–win China US, win–win social harmony." Everything is "win–win."

The idea goes to the Ricardian notion of comparative advantage: that if you give up something that someone can do better and more cheaply, then you can move into something else.

Look at the "win–win" and you can see how it has worked. It has definitely worked in the developing world. Per capita income exploded. But in the major countries of the developed world, the share of labor is at a record low, the share going to the owners of capital is at a record high. So who wins? Especially in the US, where for the median guy in the middle, real wages have stayed unchanged for a decade.

We all want to stay on the globalization side of the spectrum driven by trade liberalization, low inflation, low interest rates, strong profits, and benign currency adjustments. But if we don't watch ourselves and we let politicians do stupid things, we get a much tougher scenario called localization.

My advice: Don't take globalization for granted. Don't lapse into the mindless "win–win" mantra and pretend that everybody accepts it. As voters around the world and their elected politicians are now articulating, they don't get it. And the ones who think they do, don't like it. It is incumbent on us to come up with a better defense of why this may really be "win–win."

The risk, however, is that if politicians get a hold of things, we could be flipped toward localization, and that could be a total, unmitigated disaster. The body politic has spoken in Washington and increasingly in Europe. Over the three years to early 2008, the US

(continued)

Congress introduced 45 separate pieces of legislation that were aimed at imposing trade sanctions on China. In 2007, two of the votes passed major Senate committees—by overwhelming bipartisan majorities. The drumbeat is getting louder and louder as far as protectionism is concerned.

No nation can take its place for granted in the world economy. Back in the mid-1800s, the world's biggest economy was China. China has now regained about half the share it has lost. India has regained about 35 percent to 40 percent of its share. The US on this basis peaked in the early 1950s and has been moving down slowly ever since.

The question you have to ask is, what are the next 20 to 30 to 40 years going to look like? Will it be the Asian century? If so, how is the world going to respond to the ongoing, rapid, impressive development in this part of the world? What does it mean for the US, Europe, and Japan?

Are we going to figure out better ways to cope with an increasingly integrated global economy, or are we going to push back the clock and fight to hold on to our share by imposing trade barriers, sanctions or protectionism? These are all tough and important questions.

Right now we are going through a tough cycle; a full blown financial crisis and a major downturn in the world economy. But it's still a cycle. As a cycle, we will see a recovery, but the character of the recovery—its vigor and sustainability and what it means for globalization and its role in this region—is still open to question. As the world's most important beneficiary of globalization, Asia has much at stake in this debate.

Notes

1 Thomas L. Friedman, *The World Is Flat: A Brief History Of The Twenty-first Century* (New York: Straus and Giroux, 2005), 205.
2 Charles Gave, Louis-Vincent Gave, Anatole Kaletsky, Steven Vannelli, *The End Is Not Nigh* (Hong Kong: GaveKal Research, 2007), 3–6.
3 Ibid.
4 Ibid.
5 Stiglitz, Joseph E., *Globalization and Its Discontents* (W.W. Norton & Company), 93–118, 206–30.
6 ibid., 236–9.

Chapter 3

China and the Go West Policy

In the late 1970s, China's then Premier Deng Xiaoping developed a two-pronged strategy for opening his country to the West: first the eastern coastal regions would be developed, then it would be the turn of western China. China has pretty well stuck to the plan. In the late 1990s, the first phase was declared a success, and in 2000 the Go West policy was officially launched under Premier Jiang Zemin. The official aim was to close the economic and social disparities between eastern and western China. There was certainly some work to do. According to the Asian Development Bank (ADB), in 1998, the per capita GDP of western China was about one-third that of the Eastern region. Poverty was around 14 percent—seven times higher than in the east.

The program focuses on 11 provinces: Chongqing, Sichuan, Guizhou, Yunnan, Shaanxi, Gansu, Qinghai, Ningxia, Xinjiang, Inner Mongolia, and Guanxi, with a specific focus on Chengdu, which was given special status under the central government (see figure 3.1). These areas represent 25 percent of China's population, but only 15 percent of its GDP.

The Go West policy's goal has been to ensure stability through economic growth by focusing on:

Figure 3.1: Western region of China

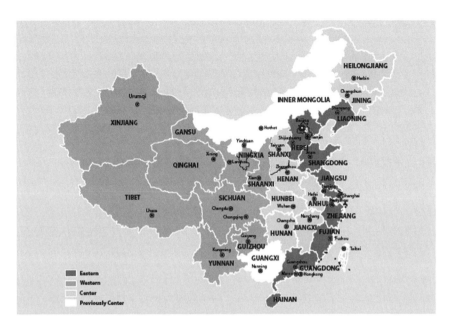

Source: Asian Development Bank 2002, The 2020 Project: Policy Support in the People's Republic of China, figure 1-1, p. 4.

- investing in public infrastructure and providing fiscal incentives;
- providing subsidized bank credit for private investment; and
- setting up special economic zones (SEZs) for export and foreign investment.

So far, it has made considerable progress. Growth has focused not only on foreign direct investment (FDI) but also on directing government resources toward the western region. Building infrastructure is one of China's strengths, as we have seen in the development of the eastern region and the 2008 Olympic games. Just on the transport side, a number of major infrastructure projects have been completed or are near completion, such as the Yunnan Expressway, the Southern Yunnan Road Development Project, the Guangxi Roads Development Project, the Guangxi Roads Development II Project, and the Yunnan Dali–Lijiang Railway Project.

  Each has been funded by the ADB together with the People's Republic of China. The ADB alone has provided approximately

Figure 3.2: Used FDI in western China

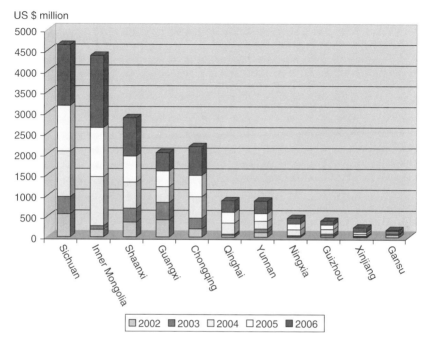

Source: Economist Intelligence Unit, April 2007.

$1.2 billion. That's a considerable sum, but the results of such investments are becoming tangible. By 2010, the government expects to have an additional 22,000 miles of new roads and 2,500 miles of new railways. Moreover, a natural gas pipeline originating in Xinjiang and stretching to Shanghai has come into operation, costing the central government $24 billion in investment.

While building up the infrastructure of the western provinces is an important factor in forging a stronger relationship with the eastern provinces, the ultimate goal is to attract investment from both foreign and local companies. Since the inception of the Go West policy, there have been substantial increases in FDI there, but those increases are still significantly smaller than in the eastern, more developed region. Figure 3.2 shows the increases in used FDI in the provinces targeted by the Go West policy.

As you can see, investment varies considerably by year and location. Some areas have been much more successful than others, thanks in large part to the efforts of local and provincial governments.

Those major global corporations that have made significant investments in recent years have been drawn not only by incentives but also pools of readily available talent. Intel invested $375 million in its Chengdu plant, and created up to 600 jobs after its inception there in 2005. This is just the beginning, according to Intel's website. There are plans to expand to four factories with a total of 600,000 square feet and two general-purpose buildings with a total of 200,000 square feet. Part of the reason for choosing this site was the availability of a well-educated workforce.

Similarly, Ford Motor Company has set up in Chongqing. The initial agreement was to invest up to $1 billion over several years to expand the current facility and ramp up production. In 2006, Ford launched production of the Volvo S40 as it continued to expand its capabilities in this rapidly growing city. In 2007, two additional models were added to the production line: the Volvo C70 and S80.

Other key investors include Boeing, Caterpillar, Goodyear, Alcoa, Unisys, and Microsoft, while many local companies are also actively pursuing opportunities in the hinterlands. As the economy in the West has grown, so has workers' pay. Urban wages in Chongqing averaged $126 a month, up 60 percent since 2002, according to interviews with several local businesspeople reported in the US in July 2007 on the Public Broadcasting Service's *Nightly Business Report.*

Many question the effectiveness of the Go West policy. But while the gains may initially appear modest, it is clear something is working, and the policy's objectives are being met. Used FDI increased 100 percent there between 2002 and 2006, according to the *Economist Intelligence Unit.* The hope is that, with investment by high-profile companies and strong marketing, the western region will continue to grow significantly over the next decade and close the gap with eastern China. Look at the evidence of China itself: since opening its doors, it has grown into a global player.

From factory to player

After Deng Xiaoping's Southern Tour of China in the late 1970s, the world witnessed a strong and rapid growth in the country's economy. This has been achieved through phased foreign investments in different industries, initially manufacturing but now including financial institutions, plus the use of massive foreign investment, resources, and technology to develop local business and talent that is globally competitive.

But economic growth, however impressive, also brings its own challenges. In early 2000, millions of workers were laid off during the consolidation of many inefficient state-owned enterprises (SOEs). The Go West policy and the appreciation of the yuan forced many low-tech, low-margin companies to move west or to close down altogether. With the country's manufacturing industry facing deregulation, along with overcapacity, the appreciation of the yuan and squeezed profit margins, the need for less competition and higher profit potential gave rise to a new breed of Chinese company. These were not content just to operate locally: they had the motivation and scale to expand into global markets. And they had official backing.

In China's most recent five-year plan, the government included among its goals the creation of worldwide brands. This led Beijing to relax financial controls on outward direct investment to encourage Chinese companies to make overseas investments. It's all part of a "Go Global" strategy to diversify and take advantage of international opportunities. This expansion is being backed by the policies of government agencies such as the National Development & Reform Commission (NDRC) and the State Administration of Foreign Exchange (SAFE), and the results are beginning to show. According to government statistics, Chinese companies spent $18.76 billion in direct foreign investment in 2007. They then eclipsed that by spending $19.34 billion in the first three months of 2008 alone (www.english .gov.cn, May 12, 2008).

As with the Japanese and Koreans before them, Chinese companies are building on their export origins to become global players in industries ranging from electronics to automobiles. Take the example of Haier. It has successfully become a global brand, with new and innovative products going into developed countries such as the US and into developing countries as well. Other companies have attempted to acquire overseas firms as a shortcut to creating a global presence. Lenovo's purchase of IBM's Personal Computer Division, Shanghai Automotive Industrial Corp.'s acquisition of the majority of Korea's SsangYong, China National Petroleum Corp.'s acquisition of

PetroKazakhstan, and unsuccessful bids by Haier for Maytag, Shanghai Auto for MG Rover, CNOOC for Unocal, and Huawei for 3Com all show that the intent is there, as does approval for the Industrial & Commercial Bank of China Ltd. (ICBC) to buy a 20 percent stake in the Standard Bank Group Ltd. of South Africa.

However, Chinese corporations overseas face their own share of challenges brought about by globalization, such as tariff and anti-dumping controls imposed by the US and European Union (EU). Political pressure in some countries has also resulted in unsuccessful foreign acquisitions, such as CNOOC's bid for Unocal, and apparent delays in getting permits to open Chinese banks overseas. These also serve as protests against China's "closed" financial markets.

Overall, it is not easy for Chinese companies to win in the global marketplace, where there is increasing international competition, deregulation, instant communication, and free markets. Whether they go global through organic growth, joint ventures, or mergers and acquisitions, they must overcome significant challenges to compete against established foreign firms, including those within China.

To do this, they need to build up strengths. China's manufacturing industry should look to high technology, low energy consumption, and environmental protection when improving its competitiveness world-wide. It is also important to secure a talent pool skilled in global marketing, management and operations. Global partnerships and acquisitions can help here, but post-merger integration poses challenges as well as bringing benefits. Mindsets may need adapting. According to Chen Shaopeng, President, Lenovo Emerging Market Group and Senior Vice President, Lenovo Group (who is quoted at length further into this chapter), "to have a successful postmerger integration, one should have the right corporate culture to manage the cultural differences and egos."

Today, China is a nation with robust economic and political power. It holds records for the continuous growth of its GDP, export income and foreign reserves, which were the highest in the world in 2007 (see figure 3.3). China also overtook the US in manufacturing output in 2006, while becoming one of the largest foreign investors in the US. Chinese investments are moving from US Treasury bonds to US corporations directly or indirectly, as through Blackstone private equity. As China grows economically, so does its influence.

Figure 3.3: China GDP per capita (PPP)

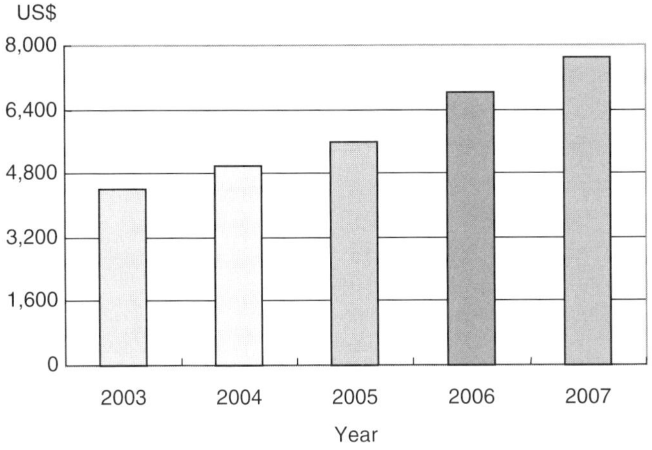

Year

Source: CIA World Factbook.

But, as we will argue, there are challenges attached to its new position on the world stage.

Sustainability

China's rapid growth has raised questions about whether it is sustainable. The evidence suggests that it isn't when applying the triple bottom line (TBL), developed by John Elkington of the SustainAbility strategy consultancy as a way of viewing sustainability based on existing economic, social, and environmental factors.

China, as the world's third-largest economy, has relied on its exports and the globalization of trade as the main means of achieving its economic goals. Its share of world trade, according to the IMF, surpasses that of Japan, India, and the ASEAN-4 countries. However, as an export-driven economy, it inevitably suffered during the global economic downturn in 2008. Underlying factors in the Chinese economy, including its employment rate and its domestic consumer consumption, aggravate its hopes for continued high growth.

As highlighted by Stephen S. Roach, Chairman of Morgan Stanley Asia, who is quoted further at the end of this chapter, China's SOEs have laid off approximately 65 million workers, and millions more are afraid of losing their jobs. This was the situation before the 2008 downturn. The "iron rice bowl" mentality caused by workers' dependence on state-owned companies for their livelihood is no longer relevant.

Furthermore, because of the unstable unemployment situation, people are saving out of fear, a development that has a negative impact on personal consumption rates. According to data provided by Morgan Stanley Research, personal consumption as a percentage of GDP decreased from about 65 percent in 1952 to about 35 percent in 2006. This challenges the general view of China as the next consumer-based economy. More importantly, it raises important questions about the country's future economic sustainability.

Look closely at the social environment, as part of the TBL, and there may also be a concern from a sustainability perspective. China has been challenged by the international community, in particular the US, because of its human rights track record, especially its treatment of minority groups, religious groups, and political prisoners.

Internal protests have certainly been on the rise. Ministry of Public Security figures show participants in protests grew from 73,000 in 1994 to three million in 2003 and 3.76 million in 2004.

Further, China's seventy-second ranking in the Transparency International Corruption Perception Index may suggest that money received for projects is not being shared among the poorer population, which could widen the gap between the rich and the poor—resulting in future social unrest.

On the environmental front, China's growth rate has been matched by pollution created by its manufacturing industries. In addition, the country's thirst for energy and its byproducts has changed the ecosystem significantly, if not permanently. The Three Gorges Dam project is a prominent example of the environmental impact of development on local communities. Air pollution in Beijing, highlighted as it prepared for the 2008 Olympics, is another indicator of China's environmental sustainability.

An analysis of China's sustainability through TBL shows the country has some serious hurdles in front of it. These were perhaps best summed up by Premier Wen Jiabao's statement in March 2007 that macro conditions were "unstable, unbalanced, uncoordinated, and unsustainable." That comes from the top.

Growing political influence

While there is debate outside the country about some aspects of China's role on the world stage and, periodically, about its actions domestically, several mainland executives in the Kellogg-HKUST Executive MBA class (intake 2007–08) felt strongly that the country was not getting enough credit for its actions.

They wrote: "Over the past 10 years, several challenges have presented themselves in Asia, including the Asian Financial Crisis in 1997, SARS in 2003, the Southern China Storm in early 2008, and the disastrous earthquakes a few months later. These potentially devastating issues did not stop China's economic growth, nor did they lessen its political influence. On the contrary, China's economic growth has even accelerated, clearing the way for an equally sharp increase in regional and global political influence."

The executives used as an example the North Korean nuclear crisis in 2006, which began when China's reclusive neighbor declared its first successful development of nuclear warheads.

"By facilitating discussions between North Korea and the US, China helped ease tensions and rescued the situation from further deterioration. China has actively coordinated the six-party talks and pushed resumption of these discussions to achieve a realistic and effective way to resolve the nuclear issue. By effectively inserting itself into the situation, China is playing a major role in the Korean Peninsula issue and has helped minimize the threat of a global nuclear disaster," they wrote.

The executives see this as part of a wider picture: "China has persistently adhered to its own principles, namely, respecting the independence of an existing country, and does not interfere with the internal affairs of other countries. Unlike some countries with powerful economies, China does not follow the traditional rules of the powerful. The consistency and respect shown by maintaining its own principles, regardless of the pace of growth, has won China the respect and recognition of many other countries.

"Internally, China's stability has contributed to its growing power. Since 1990, the leadership has placed stability as its first priority, and this policy has been maintained ever since. On the other hand, even though China's political influence is growing, its influence is still relatively low compared to the size of its economy. Today, there are Chinese products in every corner of the world. However, people in many countries still do not know China well, and some even misunderstand its culture."

CHEN SHAOPENG, President, Lenovo Emerging Market Group; Senior Vice President, Lenovo Group

"Cultural integration is all about trust."

At that time, Lenovo's business was much bigger than IBM's PC business on the mainland. For a leader from the buy side like me, it would have been easy to just think about integrating all the [IBM] business into Lenovo's functions and then run the business like before.

But my team and I were very careful to discover what was the best way to integrate the business. We found IBM held more, larger corporate accounts. Lenovo's majority business was with consumers and SMEs. We saw this as a complementary set. So we developed a strategy for the new brand.

First, we integrated all the back-end processes to give synergy and reduce costs, because those parts didn't affect the customer. We kept the customer focal point, the customer interfaces as before because those business models were different. The integration was a great success. China showed the highest growth rate that year across the world in Lenovo for the ThinkPad business we had acquired from IBM.

But it wasn't only the business operation that required our attention. We also started to integrate the teams and their cultures.

I believed it necessary to show respect for the past. I introduced a new approach for the management team. When we had meetings to discuss strategy and the best approach to integration, I always asked the incumbent managers to be open minded and share all their insights. Then I would ask the leader from IBM to make the final remark.

In China, the big boss always has the final word. But we changed that approach. And although the IBM leader had the last say, I felt able to be open about things myself.

Later, when the integration was finished, I received a lot of feedback from the IBM team members. They felt respected and trusted and have remained in the team until now.

I was careful, however, to stay true to one Chinese tradition. The project team and I wanted to show a warm welcome to the IBM team, which was very small when compared to the rest of us.

In the first days after they moved into Lenovo's headquarters, everyone's desk had a small basin of flowers. We also held

(*continued*)

welcoming ceremonies at every location throughout the different segments of the building.

Maybe some of you think this is stupid, but these are matters of great importance in mainland China.

Then there was the business of the chairs. During the integration process, we found Lenovo's chairs were different from IBM's. Theirs were more comfortable for the back and helped improve productivity. Beforehand, we didn't know . . . I didn't know the difference between these chairs.

But once we found out, we quickly transferred all the chairs within the Lenovo building. We changed more than 5,000 chairs. We thought this was better for the employees. When we find something is best practice, we instantly implement it. That's our culture and our style.

During this journey, however, sometimes my Eastern colleagues faced conflict with their Western colleagues. The Westerners knew more about the rest of the world, and they had experience in running a global business. We needed a common culture that ran across the world.

Now the whole team has consensus. A combination proved the best way, not that this or that side was the best. We prefer to introduce best practices from every side. Like myself, I changed my mind a lot. I'm a pioneer, introducing a lot of best practices from the rest of the world. I have a lot of appreciation for my western colleagues. This is the key.

If the buy side believed strongly that the original culture should be dominant, that would definitely lead to failure. Cultural integration is all about trust. How you trust others and how they trust you. Until now everything has run smoothly, but we have not totally completed the journey.

STEPHEN ROACH, Chairman, Morgan Stanley Asia Pacific

"Not spending, but saving out of fear"

You can't keep growing an economy solely by adding to its supply and using that supply, or capacity, to push goods out into global markets, without stimulating your own domestic economy. It's a

(continued)

(continued)

classic strategy of economic development that you start as an exporter. Then you shift to import substitution and eventually grow your internal markets.

China is trying to do this. But it has one huge challenge that most developing countries have not had to handle on such a scale: China is transitioning from a centrally planned system to market-based socialism. The key moving piece of this transition has been SOEs. Closing down inefficient, massive SOEs and replacing them with privately owned, corporatized, mixed enterprises are key to this ownership transition.

Over the past decade, SOE reform has led to the laying-off of more than 65 million workers. If you have worked for an SOE and you lose your job, you don't just lose your labor income. You also lose your iron rice bowl: housing, medical care, pensions, education, in some cases food and clothing allowances.

Moreover, millions more are afraid they may be next. This has led to a huge tendency toward precautionary savings, saving out of fear—knowing that the state is not going to be there to provide you with the basic necessities of your life today and when you retire.

That's why the consumption share is so low in China. Chinese officials know that; first and foremost, to sustain a broad-based consumer culture, build a safety net, focus on funding a social security system, focus on pensions, focus on unemployment insurance, worker retraining.

The Chinese government is committed to this. The eleventh five-year plan, enacted three years ago, is filled with provisions aimed in that direction. But any progress has been disappointingly slow. That's a key structural aspect of sustainability in China. It needs to be dealt with before China can feel more confident about the longer-term prognosis.

Chapter 4

Achieving Stability in a Volatile World

At the time of writing, half the world seemed consumed by a growing sense of gloom. A crumbling away of a section of the US credit market in mid-2007 opened up networks of deep cracks throughout the housing, banking, and credit systems in the US, Europe, and Asia, raising risk, freezing credit, jolting stockmarkets, and dissolving wealth. While the world in the early half of the decade celebrated apparently relentless globalization and the interlinking of financial markets, that interdependency is now seen as a risk.

In the late-1990s the world watched southeast Asia's financial crises with some shaking of heads. In 2008, it was America's profligacy that became the target of criticism. This chapter looks at how leaders in their field see the prospects for Asia, what destabilizing consequences these economic shocks may bring, and how we as leaders in Asia can prepare ourselves.

Our perspective is largely China—in our study group, five out of seven are ethnically Chinese and speak one or more Chinese dialects. One of us is a PRC national. The other two group members are expats based in Hong Kong and China. We live daily in the presence of China, and for us, when someone says "Asia," we think first and foremost of

China. So we make no apology for focusing on China as an emerging global power.

Recent global economic forecasts and decoupling

China is poised at the brink of a momentous shift in its trading environment. Its largest single export market, the US, is crumbling at the edges. One of the challenges that business and political leaders in China face is the prediction of how much impact a US downturn, or a severe slowdown, will have on the Chinese economy.

Is the Chinese producer still joined at the hip with the US consumer? Or is the US umbilical cord shriveling in the wake of new hands that feed China's export dollars from Asia, the EU, and emerging markets? The decoupling debate has been furrowing the brows of business leaders for some time now, and still the divergent schools of thought continue to, well, diverge.

Of course a decoupling of the Chinese economy from the US economy does not entail absolute independence and stability, so that China would be completely unaffected by a US recession. The real question is whether the coming of age of China as a global economic force has afforded it the ability to soften the blow significantly.

The concept of decoupling appears to be incongruent with globalization. As the world economy becomes increasingly integrated, with the tendrils of trade and finance intertwining across the globe, business cycles should inherently become more synchronized. Stephen Roach, Chairman of Morgan Stanley Asia and a vocal critic of the decoupling theory, argues that these growing cross-border linkages inevitably tether the rest of the world to the two dominant powerhouses of the global economy, China and the US.

According to Roach, for an economy to decouple from the US, it must have a self-sustaining domestic demand, a diversified export mix and policy autonomy.[1] China's private consumption as a percentage of GDP was 38 percent in 2006, which is well below the world average of 59 percent. The US is China's largest single export destination, comprising a consistent 21 percent of China's total exports over the past decade.[2] The scope of China's fiscal policies is limited by its history of budget deficits, and currency policy is also restricted by a quasi-peg to the US dollar. If anything, the Beijing government actively perpetuates a dependence on the US by retaining the quasi-peg, which suppresses the *yuan* at an artificially low valuation to preserve export competitiveness with the US while at the same time depressing domestic private consumption.[3] In the context of Roach's prerequisites for decoupling, China appears to strike out on all three accounts.

In January 2008, the decoupling theory was further condemned by a ferocious two-day slide in the Shanghai Stock Exchange of 11.98 percent or RMB 3.18 trillion. This freefall in China was triggered by reports of a looming US recession spawned by the US subprime crisis, which insidiously and unavoidably infected the banking industry globally. China had admitted that it was not immune to the subprime crisis. This manifestation of the disease stung not only the government and big business, but also private investors.

Fearless proponents of decoupling, such as Arthur Kroeber, director of Dragonomics, rose from the rubble and explained that the stockmarket only represents a fraction of China's economic activity, and that the Shanghai slide was a knee-jerk reaction typical of new markets with high levels of speculation. Furthermore, the theory of decoupling should be regarded as a long-term phenomenon, which should not be discounted by short-term volatility.

The strongest argument for decoupling rests in the premise that the insatiable consumption of the US can be replaced by the rest of the world. If this is the case, then China's production push will merely be diverted to other countries and its economy will continue to flourish, regardless of a US downturn. The EU and intra-regional trade in Asia have become significantly stronger and continue to grow in stature. The EU as a collective has surpassed the US as China's greatest export destination, accounting for more than 21 percent of China's total exports. China's exports to emerging econo-mies like Russia, India, and Brazil grew more than 60 percent in dollar terms in the year ended January 2008, constituting half of China's total exports, whereas export growth to the US fell to only 5 percent.[4] This demand has been stimulated by the growth in productivity, domestic incomes and spending in these markets. Consumer spending in emerging economies rose three times as fast as that of developed economies.[5]

Regardless of the concept of decoupling, weaker demand from the US will inevitably lead to further weakening in export sector growth, already in decline, from 30 percent in mid-2005 to 10 percent at the time of writing. Recent stories of factory closures in low-end manufacturing zones in south China are a clear sign of this. Analysis from Deutsche Bank notes that because of labor productivity rises of 15 percent annually, the sector no longer creates jobs, and *yuan* appreciation and rising costs of inputs, especially labor, have shrunk margins. With 11 percent of China's labor force currently employed in the export sector, a drop in export growth may have big economic implications.

Many China exporters have been seeking alternative export destinations as a result of US protectionist policies and the appreciation of the yuan against the US dollar.[6] To some extent, the roles of other countries as economic centers and trading partners have grown in importance in the face of a shrinking US economy. However the impact is hard to quantify now. As the next decade unfurls, a much clearer picture will materialize.

China's domestic consumption is the fulcrum on which the whole decoupling debate is balanced. Over 95 percent of China's 2007 growth of 11.2 percent can be attributed to domestic demand.[7] More than half the domestic investment is attributable to infrastructure and property, with less than 15 percent dedicated to the export sector. This suggests that return from investment should remain robust, even in the face of adversity in the US. However, private consumption as a percentage of GDP languished at a record low of 38 percent in 2005 and 2006. This contrasts starkly with US personal consumption, which has risen steadily for the past few decades to more than 70 percent of GDP. According to Roach, "consumption support is absolutely critical for an economy to prosper on its own."[8]

Being the most populous country in the world, coupled with a powerhouse economy, China's private consumption has tremendous potential. The middle class has reached 80 million, and is forecast to hit 700 million by 2020.[9] Disposable income per capita for urban residents increased by more than 17 percent in 2007.[10] In real dollar terms, Chinese private consumption has been climbing steadily, from less than RMB5 trillion in 2001 to RMB7.8 trillion in 2006.[11] Although it has not attained a level that would comfortably sustain China's economy, indicators show it is heading in the right direction.

The absence of clear evidence indicating that China has decoupled from the US economy seems to suggest that the two economies are still closely linked, and therefore China is susceptible to the perils of a US recession. Prime Minister Wen Jiabao's ominous warning that 2008 would be a "most difficult year for the economy" as a result of international uncertainties and domestic issues echoes this harsh reality. [12]

China, however, is planting the seeds to achieve greater independence. What we are seeing now may be the genesis of the decoupling process. To facilitate this process, it is important for business and political leaders to embrace the challenge of increasing domestic private consumption and bolstering trade ties with the rest of the world beyond the US, especially the EU, Asia, and emerging economies.

Yuan revaluation and China's role in global trade

The clichés have become well-worn—that China is the world's factory and its undervalued currency is a form of export subsidy. China's currency has been a scapegoat for two ills—one is the loss of manufacturing jobs in the US and Europe to Chinese exporters, and the other, related one is the trade deficit. The US trade deficit with China, at more than 30 percent of the total in early 2008, makes it an obvious target, but it is only the largest portion of a trade imbalance with a total of 40 countries. US politicians have in their sights legislation that would impose tariffs on a host of low-cost goods from China in an attempt to redress the trade imbalance. As Roach states: "This could be a policy blunder of monumental proportions."

Roach argues that the root of the problem is the chronically low rate of savings by the US consumer that requires the US to maintain large current account and trade deficits to attract capital. Trade sanctions would only have the effect of raising the cost of goods, for example the $18 billion in merchandise that Wal-Mart imports from China, amounting to a tax on the consumer, and simply diverting trade to other countries, without significantly changing the overall picture for the US. Even worse, China is currently the US's largest creditor, buying up dollar-backed assets to maintain its fixed exchange rate. The effect of this is to maintain low US interest rates. Revaluing the *yuan* would bring with it a reduction in those US dollar holdings and obviously a further drop in the dollar's value. A gradual pace of appreciation, bringing a gradual sell-off of dollar assets, is much better for the stability of the dollar. So Roach asks, is China's undervalued currency a subsidy to its own industries, or a subsidy to the US consumer?

Roach points to another striking fact—of the merchandise entering the US from China, only 20 percent actually originates there. Roach explains the concept of a "Pan-Asian supply chain" centered around China. Restricting trade with China would have a knock-on effect for Japan, Korea, and other Asian countries that are part of the chain. While China has a trade surplus with the US and EU, it has a deficit with many other countries. And the "Chinese manufacturer" is also somewhat of a misnomer—a significant portion of exports from China are products made by US subsidiaries.

No doubt Roach's viewpoint, echoed throughout many articles, is unpopular with many in the US. Roach offers an example of thought leadership—speaking out against popular, and misguided, conceptions of Asia—which is sorely needed at a time when the world economy is on the defensive and under pressure to retrench itself.

For its part, China has had strong political interests for keeping currency appreciation in check. A rapid appreciation of the yuan would damage the health of export industries in the coastal areas and deal a blow to China's still embryonic capital markets, which have few instruments for hedging currency risk. Through most of 2007 China appeared to be sticking to its stated target of 3–5 percent appreciation per year.

However, maintaining an undervalued currency has become increasingly unsustainable for China, and its rationale is also diminishing. China's economy is far less dependent on export-led growth than in the previous decade, and imports are rising, particularly of much needed commodities. Domestic consumption is also picking up: in February 2008, *The Economist* quoted a study showing that in 2007 consumption accounted for a bigger share of GDP growth than investment for the first time in seven years.

The price that China has paid for sterilizing the *yuan* is that it is becoming a cause of instability. Analysts at Deutsche Bank have noted that by the fourth quarter of 2007, the pace of appreciation seemed to have quickened to a 6–9 percent range. This is the inevitable result of ballooning foreign reserves, the relatively slow pace of liberalization of capital controls, rising inflation, and growth in money supply. According to a prediction in *The Economist* Country Report for China, the exchange rate will average RMB6.45:US$1 by 2011.

Obviously, exchange rates have a direct impact on all businesses operating in China. In past years, relatively low domestic inflation and a fixed exchange rate meant that companies earning dollars and spending *yuan* could manage margins. Now the squeeze is noticeable.

The dangers of inflation

At the end of January 2008, Premier Wen Jiabao told the media: "2008 is the most difficult year for the economy." Why did he say that? Was it because there was a great deal of uncertainty in the international environment, and at the same time China was facing many new domestic difficulties and challenges?

A month later, in his government work report delivered to the annual National People's Congress (NPC), Wen urged his officials to monitor closely the risks of international imbalances, protectionism, and the problems in the US financial sector. But he made it clear that the top political priority was curbing consumer price inflation in China, which hit an 11-year high of 7.1 percent in January. "The primary task for macroeconomic regulation this year is to prevent fast economic growth from becoming overheated growth and keep the structural price increases from turning into significant inflation," he said.

Wen promised the government would maintain a prudent fiscal policy and a tight monetary policy to keep consumer inflation about 4.8 percent for 2008, which is the same as the actual inflation rate for 2007, but much higher than the official target of 3 percent for that year. However, Stephen Green of Standard Chartered Bank, quoted in *The Economist*, said that Wen's target was "dangerously unattainable."

A few factors are fueling China's inflation, including wages and rising prices for raw materials. Another major contributor is the agricultural sector. The snowstorms that crippled the country at the beginning of 2008 amplified inflationary pressure in this sector. Figures from the *China Daily* showed that by mid-February some 26 million acres of crops out of a total of 388 million acres had been affected by the snowstorms, leading to the need to import grains. Sixty-three million poultry, four million pigs, 1.38 million sheep, and 393,000 cows died as a result of the disaster, bringing about higher meat prices. The Agricultural Price Index rose 18 percent during

January, 14 times faster than the monthly average increase over the previous six months.

The political backlash from rampant inflation could be overwhelming. Wen experienced the effects firsthand as he stood next to his late mentor Zhao Zi Yang, when Zhao tried to calm protesting students in Tiananmen Square in June 1989. The student demonstrations were initially sparked by worries over inflation before they gathered momentum and grew into a protest against corruption and a call for political reform.

To maintain social harmony and stability, Mr. Wen announced in his NPC speech that the government would earmark funds to promote the development of education, science and technology, medical care, social welfare, environmental protection, rural economic growth, and the narrowing of regional and social gaps. According to a *South China Morning Post* report of March 6, 2008, spending in these areas will increase by some 17–45 percent. While alleviating political pressure, this increased spending is likely to intensify China's increasing inflationary pressure.

In this context, there is the further risk that inflation could turn into a spiral when the expectation of inflation becomes a self-fulfilling prophecy. In a recent survey carried out by the People's Bank of China, 65 percent of respondents expected higher inflation, compared with the 50 percent normally seen. A Deutsche Bank study has shown that panic buying or stockpiling of goods tends to occur when the CPI enters the critical range of 7–15 percent. A study carried out by the IMF reinforces this inflationary spiral by showing that inflation expectation tends to explain 60 percent of future inflation.

If rampant inflation continues, the Chinese government may further tighten its monetary and fiscal policies and extend administrative price controls over a wider range of goods and services. These policies were typical during the 1987–88 and 1993–94 high inflationary periods. The stockmarket is bound to react negatively; for example, in June 1993 and June 1994, the Shanghai Composite Index dropped by 53 percent. The mainland stockmarket fell during Wen's delivery of his NPC speech because his strong anti-inflation stance made traders believe that further monetary tightening was inevitable.

Sherman Chan, an economist at Moody's Economy.com, wrote in a research note: "China is certainly at a crossroads now—inflation risk remains on the upside, which warrants tightening measures, but a slowing global economy threatens the country's growth prospect." Whichever road the Chinese government decides to take, it is likely to be a bumpy one.

Feverish equity markets

Another phenomenon has been bubbles in the asset and equity markets. Lacking alternatives for investment, and with Chinese domestic savings fueling cheap credit from banks, companies have been engaged in a buying binge on the Shanghai and Shenzhen exchanges. Many commentators have linked low interest rates to steep rises in the stockmarket. Reports of speculative borrowing by SOEs to make illegal investments in the stockmarket and real estate regularly make the news in China. Jonathan Anderson, an economist at UBS, estimates that of the more than 40 percent rise in corporate earnings in China in 2007, about 15 percent may have been the result of one-off stockmarket gains.

The Shanghai Composite Index rose 97 percent in 2007, raising price/earnings (PE) ratios to unsustainable levels, spurred by the massive entry of relatively irrational and inexperienced individual investors. At the height of the surge, in August 2007, one million stock-trading accounts were open, the *Financial Times* reported.

The effects of this explosion in day trading by the Chinese public was seen on the ground. Executives spoken to up to early 2008 told stories of employees talking about nothing else but the market's performance, and how even low-wage workers were fixed to computer screens during lunch breaks to check prices. One employee in the company for which one writer of this chapter works told how he had made so much money from stock trading that he now worked just to keep himself busy. Such prosperity, particularly for those old enough to remember what extreme poverty feels like, is surely welcome. However, as an employer in China, this executive worries about what effects such activity, effectively a form of gambling, will have on the stability of the workforce.

Many of the hazards of China's equity markets are well known, primarily a lack of transparency and asymmetrical information that prevent the market performing its function of efficient allocation of capital. Coupled with that, China's Securities Regulatory

Commission lacks resources and powers, in some cases taking years to complete an investigation.

Market and social forces take hold

However, economic development in China often takes surprising turns. In an article from March 1, 2008, *The Economist*, quoting a Columbia Law School study, noted that the exchanges themselves may have taken on a limited role in policing listed companies through their power to rebuke companies and individuals through public notices. The study showed that public notices had the effect of lowering stock prices and had other invisible effects on the target's dealings with creditors. Foreigners often underestimate the powerful effect of public naming and shaming in China, which seems to have deep cultural roots.

This is a growing trend seen in other sectors of society—public outcry or admonition in the press as a substitute for legal sanction. It seems that whenever influential figures are seen to be abusing power or escaping responsibility, the issue becomes a firestorm spread through the Internet and local grapevine until it becomes a focus of national attention and something that the government cannot ignore.

It happened with the beating to death of an innocent bystander by thuggish city administration officials in Henan, with mining companies that have tried to avoid responsibility for fatal accidents, and with official collusion over slave labor in Hebei.

With or without official outlets, China is developing a civil society by virtue of having the world's highest ownership of mobile phones and, soon, the highest number of Internet users. China's instinctive authoritarian approach—to attempt mass censorship of the Internet—no longer works as it used to with official media. A more balanced approach that also involves management of public opinion is noticeable.

This was clearly evident in the remarkable scenes surrounding 2008's Spring Festival crisis, where both Wen Jiabao and Hu Jintao were shown tirelessly wading through crowds of stranded workers, promising to fix electricity and rail lines. That was followed by "Grandpa" Wen's almost nonstop appearances during the aftermath of the Sichuan earthquake. It is striking to see how unelected leaders of a one-party state have worked so hard to manage public opinion (especially when contrasted with George Bush's handling of Hurricane Katrina).

But the worry is that this form of reactive crisis management is precarious and unsustainable. There is a growing body of information about civil unrest in China—even the government's own published statistics (which are considered by many to be an understatement) show a 50 percent increase in disturbances between 2003 and 2005, when the figure was 87,000. In recent years, news reports have been more readily available, and the size of such disturbances, sometimes involving hundreds or thousands and resulting in deaths, would be national emergencies in most countries. Experts such as Albert Keidel of the Carnegie Endowment for International Peace identify these as mostly symptoms of rampant economic growth, stemming from a wide range of issues, but most recently, poorly compensated land expropriations. With the prospect of unemployment rising as export markets falter and inflation takes off, many of the less fortunate could become ever more dissatisfied.

In 2005, Premier Wen Jiabao told the Politburo that mishandling violent discontent could endanger China. A senior official, Chen Xiwen said that rural unrest threatened national security and acknowledged that reported cases were the "tip of the iceberg." Even influential Communist Party scholars have published a paper advocating urgent reforms in the courts and legislature to create "power balance mechanisms" and "modern civil society" composed of NGOs and religious groups. Clearly social stability, as an outgrowth of economic stability, is a key challenge. China's growth, rather than being an unstoppable juggernaut, may depend on a precarious balance.

China vs. India

India and China are often pitted against each other, as though the two are rivals for a share of the same pie. An incisive macroanalysis of the two countries by Professor Lakshman Krishnamurthi of the Kellogg School and Assistant Professor Sugandha Khandelwal of the Robert H. Smith School of Business, University of Maryland puts them in strikingly different trajectories. They demonstrate that while the two countries appeared to be at the same level of GDP throughout the

1980s, this masked huge infrastructure investments that China made in the previous decade which were slow to take effect, but began to propel China's growth exponentially in the 1990s relative to India's. Since 1991, the study has found China's annual GDP growth rate has averaged more than 9 percent per year, while India's has been 5.8 percent.

The "infrastructure gap" is glaringly obvious to any visitor to the two countries from the moment one arrives at the airport, and clearly demonstrates how China has benefited from state-driven investment. The lag has huge implications for India's foreign trade. For example, India has no ports capable of handling the current generation of large container ships, and a container leaving India for the US can expect to take six to 12 weeks. By contrast, China handles 20 percent of the world's containers through ports already equipped for the next generation of giant vessels, and those containers reach the US in only two to three weeks. The story is the same for the electricity grid, roads, urban transport and telecoms—India's investment as of 2006 was 3.6 percent of GDP compared with China's 9 percent.

This lack of physical infrastructure has been exacerbated by political agendas—India has pursued a more protectionist path, severely limiting foreign direct investment (FDI) in many areas and imposing burdens on businesses in the form of higher utility costs, taxes and duties, Byzantine regulations, and unfathomable land ownership. Not only did China wholeheartedly encourage FDI but funneled it into well-defined zones in the coastal provinces, magnifying its effects. India by contrast remains a patchwork, although belatedly it has realized the cost of the infrastructure lag, and is launching what amounts to a Marshall Plan of strategic infrastructure building.

Another stark difference is the basis for the economic activity in the two countries. In China, manufacturing dominates, with 49.5 percent of GDP composed of industry and 39.5 percent services. India is almost a mirror image, with 28.4 percent industry and 55 percent services, putting the service component in India close to that of G7 nations (typically 60–70 percent). However, while many think of India's role in global BPO services, this comprises a relatively tiny part of the service sector. Most of this share goes to retailing, a highly fragmented sector in India—as Krishnamurthi says, India is a "nation of shopkeepers." From this, it follows that India's GDP growth comes predominantly from domestic consumption, while China is still mainly from exports.

But other macro indicators favor India. India's banks are far healthier than China's measured by the ratio of nonperforming loans and return on assets. Its financial markets are more efficient, transparent, and underpinned by an independent legal system.

Demographics is where the differences with China may have profound effects in the future. One huge advantage India has is language—English is widely spoken in India at many levels of society. India's population is relatively better educated (8 percent in tertiary education compared with 5 percent for China) and this education is judged to be more relevant to India's needs. Certainly, it is commonplace to hear executives reporting that Indian employees can be sent almost anywhere in the world because they can communicate and adapt well, whereas their Chinese counterparts fare poorly.

The other, longer-term trend is that while China's population is aging, India's is getting younger—in Krishnamurthi's study, by 2015, India will have 31 percent of its population under 14 years old and 16 percent over 50, meaning that potentially there will be a huge reserve of working-age population to support dependents. By contrast, by the same year, China's over-50 population will number more than 32 percent as opposed to only 13 percent under 14, almost a total reversal of India's, meaning the working population will increasingly stagger under the burden of aging parents. For India, the challenge is to find work for this population. Ironically, what it needs is growth in the low-wage manufacturing sector that China currently dominates. But this may not happen. India's exports of services are unlikely to grow sufficiently, nor does it suit a mainly low-skilled workforce. On pure labor costs alone, India should already be drawing manufacturing away from China, because it is nearly four times cheaper. But again, it is the infrastructure gap that prevents this reserve from being tapped efficiently. Consequently, social unrest caused by unemployment and unequal opportunity looms as large for India as for China.

Malaysia, Indonesia, and Singapore

As Asia becomes increasingly dominated by the two emerging giant economies of India and China, the rest of the continent is in danger of being left behind. One no longer hears about the "tiger economies" of Southeast Asia, which were much heralded in the 1980s and 1990s.

It seems that the tigers got crushed between the awaking dragon and the marching elephant.

Although this cluster of nations has, on the whole, recovered from the Asian financial crisis of 1997, they could do nothing to compete with the large, cheap, and educated labor pool of the two most populous nations on Earth. Moreover, instead of strategically planning to find a niche for themselves in this new world order, they are focused inward, protecting their own turfs, and becoming embroiled in their internal politics.

One notable exception is Singapore, whose government, despite criticisms of being autocratic and undemocratic, has always been forward-thinking in its economic planning. It has created a niche for itself by moving away from head-to-head competition with Hong Kong as the financial center of Asia. Instead, it is now reinventing itself as an R&D center for the biotech and other knowledge-based industries. It is the beneficiary of the US's policy on stem-cell research, attracting the world's top 10 stem-cell research scientists in the past two years.

Malaysia recovered from the 1997 crisis and, with a smooth transition of power from the long-ruling Mahathir Mohamad to Abdullah Badawi as prime minister in 2003, it seemed to be a beacon of orderly change in the region. With a promise to root out corruption, this hope carried Badawi to a landslide mandate in the elections in the following year. However, the promise turned out to be hollow as corruption worsened. Instead of policy reforms to increase the country's competitiveness, the administration revived the affirmative action policies that favor the Malays. Instead of preparing the country to make a mark in a fast-changing Asia, the administration was marked by its inaction and politicizing of race and religion.

The disenchantment and dissatisfaction of all the races were clearly registered in the election results of March 8, 2008, when the ruling coalition clung to power by the slimmest margin in the country's history. That the ruling coalition squandered a landslide victory to the largest reversal it has seen is a significant shift in the political mood of the country. Viewed optimistically, one could say that democracy has come of age in this 50-year-old nation. However, a long period of stability comes to an end as its political and economic future is now unknown. Without a two-thirds majority and with five states in opposition hands, the ruling Barisan coalition will find it difficult to govern.

Ten years after overthrowing Suharto, Indonesia is still struggling to find stability. On Suharto's death in January 2008, there seemed to be a sense of nostalgia for the stability of the Suharto era despite its corruption, graft, and widespread human rights abuses. Although no longer pointing to the ethnic Chinese as scapegoats for all its ills, Indonesia is struggling to hold together as a nation of 490 ethnic groups. Graft and corruption continue to be a way of life. Separatist tensions and Islamist tendencies are always bubbling under the surface. As the third-most populous nation on earth, it has the potential to destabilize the whole region should these tensions boil over.

As these former tigers lose their roar and whimper along in their own domestic quagmire, can the countries of Indochina emerge to take their place? Vietnam is making some headway, with an industrious labor force that is benefiting from some factories relocating out of China due to the new Labor Contract Law implemented in 2008. Overall, however, with populations decimated by decades of war and no infrastructure to speak of, it is hard to see how Indochina can catch up.

Thailand

The overriding concern for Thailand is political and social instability. In 2006, Thailand surprised the world with a coup that ousted democratically-elected Prime Minister Thaksin, and saw a military council take temporary control. Some controversial economic policies followed, inspired by the king's call for a "self-sufficient society," including capital controls and compulsory licensing for drugs, which put the country under threat of US sanctions. Tourism revenues suffered, and the real estate sector also cooled, although this was partly a result of a long buildup of other factors, including oversupply. Most importantly, Thailand's image was dented.

The political situation remains in flux, overshadowed by Thaksin. His supporters and opponents continue to clash, sometimes violently, making a return to stable government uncertain for the near future. Thaksin's political style is confrontational, partisan, and populist—his political support is highly polarized between the provincial poor, who unshakably support him, and the urban elites who despise him. He established a reputation for ruthlessness with his "war on drugs," which resulted in thousands of alleged extrajudicial killings by the police, and his handling of the southern insurgency (which by all accounts Thaksin only managed to worsen).

This deadly separatist insurgency in the predominantly Muslim southern provinces remains Thailand's biggest unresolved social problem. While killings, bombings, and arson are localized and small scale for now, events such as the 2006 New Year bombings in Bangkok suggest that the problem could grow into a major terrorist threat.

Conclusion: dealing with risk and crisis by mastering the context

History is not kind to those shown to have underestimated looming disaster. However, there is rarely a penalty for those who with hindsight were found to have massively overestimated a threat. Only a few years ago, Asia was consumed by the terrifying and mysterious threat of SARS. It didn't matter that, medically, it was soon discovered that the condition was not easily transmitted and only clustered in sufferers who were in very close proximity to each other. The new disease brought out a reaction that was a throwback to medieval superstition: surgical masks were sold out, bleach became a topic worthy of discussion, handwashing stations sprang up, people rode the bus with fear in their eyes, mingling in a crowd was to gamble with mortality.

One of the team writing this chapter was fortunate enough to see the issue from several perspectives:

> I was working in Guangzhou, the presumed epicenter of the disease, yet the only mask wearers around town were those coming from Hong Kong. The locals went about their business as if nothing was happening, even with a faint air of amusement. Did we all have natural immunity? During the same period, I had to travel to my home in Thailand, where I was treated with a modicum of sympathy and a huge dose of mistrust—arriving at the airport I was herded into a pen, waiting a long time for a health check, then, wearing a mask to show that I could be one of the infected, I was virtually under house arrest, working from home and technically under emergency immigration measures, not supposed to go out. Even my wife, who is Asian, preferred that I keep my mask on.

I had difficulty breathing, but because of the mask, not from any infection.

The threat turned out to be minimal, and apart from the few who genuinely suffered, most of us have forgotten this brief episode. Yet it caused a significant dip in China's trade that year, and had a huge economic effect on many businesses.

As is often noted, in Chinese, the word "crisis" is a combination of the words "danger" and "opportunity." One might think of those "opportunists" who quickly launched designer surgical masks for the fashion conscious. Others took a more subtle approach. For example, during the epidemic the head of a law firm in Shanghai showed initiative by organizing a series of seminars for in-house counsel from leading multinationals, knowing that he had a captive audience who could not travel and, with business at a virtual standstill, were stuck for things to do. Busy lawyers who would normally be difficult to get hold of were almost grateful for the opportunity to meet each other and catch up on practice knowledge. The seminars had record attendances, and the firm gained some new clients, which it retains to this day.

In his classic book *On Becoming a Leader* (Random Century), Warren Bennis first talks about leaders who can "master the context." Instead of being driven by events, they drive them. As this chapter has outlined, short- and longer-term threats to stability are looming. And were we to write this paper at any point in the past or the future, there would of course still be threats, though different ones. This is probably even more true for those of us living in Asia, where a vast portion of humanity is experiencing a leap out of an historical legacy of poverty and joining, or even replacing, the traditional "developed" world. Such a seismic change cannot come without consequences, and the Asian leader must probably be better than most at looking through them.

The lesson from many crises, perhaps learned innately but rarely discussed, is that overreaction has an invisible cost too. While a crisis may be uncontrollable and unknowable, clear-headed leadership— to see beyond immediate headlines to opportunities lying beyond, and to master the context—may in future be seen as a distinctly Asian leadership quality.

STEPHEN ROACH, Chairman, Morgan Stanley Asia Pacific

"This is the first crisis of globalization."

There is absolutely nothing stable about what has been going on in the world economy and the global financial markets. This has come as a big shock because the conventional thinking over the past five years is that we have seen a spectacular boom in the global economy.

World economic growth in the five years to 2007—using the IMF metric—averaged about 5 percent, making it the strongest five-year period since the early 1970s. Over that period, there has been what policy makers and economists have concluded is "the great moderation."

Inflation has come down, interest rates have come down, markets have gone up. Volatility has declined. The price of some of our riskier assets soared. "The great moderation" is the antithesis of instability.

At the start of 2007, there was the belief that this was going to continue indefinitely. Dead wrong. We have seen a much tougher financial crisis than was the case 10 years ago. In many respects, this is the first crisis of globalization. It is a cross-border crisis—the contagion went from country to country.

It is also a cross-product contagion. It started with subprime, went into asset-backed commercial paper, offshore London Inter-bank Offered Rate (LIBOR) financing, residential mortgage-backed securities, auction rated notes, municipal bond markets.

You name it—any asset or any product with any semblance of risk that was priced unrealistically high was taken out. There's going to be a lot written over what is truly the first full-blown global crisis of a globalized, interdependent marketplace. Ten years ago, it was a crisis of economies. This has been a crisis of financial markets.

Like all crises, there's always a warning. Remember canaries in the coalmine? Back in the mid-1800s, someone discovered that the canary, with its beautiful melody, was highly sensitive to methane and carbon monoxide gas, which can get inadvertently released in a coal mine and immediately asphyxiate the miners.

So miners would take these birds into their coalmines, and 99 days out of 100, they would have beautiful melodious songs coming out of the cages. But every once in a while, a bird would stop singing and they would start running.

(*continued*)

As legend would have it, the canary was the first leading indicator of impending disaster. In the mid-to-late-1990s, we had a bubble in dotcom stocks. They said, it's only dotcom, so don't worry. After all, dotcom was only 6 percent of the market capitalization of US equities. The other 94 percent was thought to be fine. We can take the bursting of the dotcom bubble, and it wouldn't be a big deal. That was dead wrong.

The dotcom bubble burst in March 2000, and over the next two-and-a-half years, the entire S&P500 fell by 49 percent.

Fast-forward to August of 2007: subprime, 14 percent of securitized mortgages outstanding, collapsed. Conventional wisdom, including the US Federal Reserve, said don't worry. The other 86 percent was fine. Again, dead wrong.

The lesson is that when you have an asset bubble— and this comes from Yale professor Robert Shiller—it only takes a tear in the weakest part of the membrane to bring the entire asset class down.

That's what happened with dotcom. It has happened now with the monstrous credit bubble that has built up in the US and with it in the broader world financial markets. The challenge has been to figure out whether this is purely a financial market event, or an event that has meaningful implications for the underpinnings of the global economy.

What about the impact on Asia? When the US consumer stops buying, it's very difficult for the world to keep plowing ahead as though nothing happened. There's a view in Asia, widely shared in the US, that you've got billions of people—40 percent of the world's population is in China and India alone—that can step in to fill the void. Right? Dead wrong.

The US is a $10 trillion consumer. It's the big gorilla. China and India combined are $1.6 trillion. These are the little monkeys. The US is six times the combined share of China and India. It's not possible to conceive of a scenario where US consumption slows appreciably and the young consumers from China and India fill the void. The only consumer capable of doing it is the one least likely to do so—the European consumer.

The export share of Asia's GDP is at a record high. The internal private consumption share is at a record low. For this region to be "decoupled" from what happens in the US, those shares would have to be going in the opposite way. You would need growing support for

(continued)

(*continued*)

consumer consumption and reduced support for exports. Or at a minimum, at least you would have to have new sources of export markets apart from the US.

You can't, however, paint Asia with one brush. Some economies are better prepared to deal with an external shock. China, with a 13 percent growth rate in 2007, has a huge cushion. Maybe the downside for China is 5–6 percent, which is hardly a disaster. Conversely, for Japan, which goes into an external shock with only about 2 percent growth, that's clearly a more problematic outcome.

A US consumer-led recession is a rare, but significant development for developing Asia. I think it will lower pan-regional growth by three or four percentage points in 2009 from what it otherwise might have been.

There's no way China can avoid any impact. No country, no region in Asia is as close to relying on the globalization of trade and the expansion of its share of world trade than China. China does not get special dispensation from a global downturn.

Notes

1 Stephen Roach, "The Fallacy of Global Decoupling," October 2006. http://www.morganstanley.com/views/gef/archive/2006/20061030-Mon.html.

2 Eleonora Omarova, "Has China Decoupled from the United States?", in Rao, Janardhan, and Sisodiva, Amit Singh, *Economic Decoupling—Insights and Experiences*, chapter 12, Icfai University Press, 2009.

3 Tom Miller, "Markets Put Paid to Decoupling Theory," *South China Morning Post*, January 28, 2008.

4 *The Economist*, "The Decoupling Debate," March 6, 2008.

5 Ibid.

6 Keith Bradsher, "US Market Is Losing Its Appeal, Chinese Say," *International Herald Tribune*, April 17, 2007.

7 *The Economist*, op. cit.

8 Roach, op. cit.

9 An Hodgson, "China's Middle Class Reaches 80 Million," *Euromonitor*, July, 2007. www.euromonitor.com/Chinas_middle_class_reaches_80_million.

10 *China Daily* "Key Figures," 2008. http://www.chinadaily.com.cn/cndy/2008-01/25/content_6419558.htm.

11 Hodgson, op. cit.

12 George Wehrfritz, "The Imperfect Storm," *Newsweek*, February 2, 2008.

Chapter 5

Innovate and Lead

Innovation is a core business competency of the twenty-first century. To survive in the global economy, let alone compete and grow, businesses must innovate.

Some innovation powerhouses have emerged across Asia over the past decade, fueled by the desire to compete with both the established Japanese pioneers and the traditional innovation brands of Europe and the US. Consumer electronics and IT companies such as Korea's Samsung and LG, India's Infosys and Wipro, Taiwan's Asus and BenQ, and China's PC maker Lenovo, appliance producer Haier, TV manufacturer TCL, telecoms equipment provider Huawei, and global supply chain manager Li & Fung have all gained ground in global markets. Not coincidentally, they also increased their levels of innovation activity.

Many Asian economies recovered from the Asian currency crises in the late-1990s and evolved from being simply a source of cheap production into diverse economies with significant innovation capabilities. Many Asian governments are optimistic about their future, and are keen to keep it secure. Most significantly, China's growth has become more broad-based as the economy has opened up, and India is dismantling its traditional bureaucracy to support more entrepreneurial activity.[1]

Lim Siong-Guan, former chairman of the Singapore Economic Development Board, has said Singapore remains highly competitive through a heavy dose of "LSD (Lead, Speed, and Differentiation)," and that this recipe can encourage innovation in Asia. His country's desire to always stay in the "lead" lends a sense of urgency to its people to innovate. "Speed, through government agencies working in partnership to meet the needs of businesses, helps shorten the lead time for companies," he said, while differentiation helped to identify niche areas where few others were putting down stakes.[2]

Differentiation

Low-cost model: NANO in India

Product innovation is often thought of as either an incremental improvement in performance—speed, quality, usability, and so on—or a complete usurping of the current product status quo. Tata Motors is one company that is bucking that trend by taking seemingly old technologies and combining them to create a new product innovation—the world's most affordable car.

Historically, Ford and Volkswagen have been credited with "bringing cars to the masses" by developing cars at a price accessible to a large consumer segment—respectively, the Model T and the VW Beetle. However, neither company has managed to develop a car that is less than half the price of anything available at the time. Indian manufacturer Tata Motors, though, has produced the "1 Lakh car," named the NANO, some would say for its size as well as its price: it retails for US$2,500.

An examination of the automotive market in the US highlights just what an achievement this is. Automotive innovations in the US have typically been launched in premium car segments, for example, airbags, ABS, power steering, and tiptronic transmission. These in-novations over time made their way into the economy car segment thanks to manufacturing efficiencies and competition, often because Asian manufacturers were seeking to add more features to their cars to make them more attractive to consumers. Today's economy car comes much better equipped with innovations than 20 years ago, and at the same price. This seems like terrific news for the consumer. The same income group drives in more luxury and convenience than before. However, the question of affordability and price has not seen any comparable change.

Although India is known to have low labor costs, the NANO achieves its cost advantage specifically by leaving out all inessential automotive innovations. The result is:

- a 0.6-liter, 32-horsepower motorcycle engine
- no air-conditioning
- a steel frame, not the lighter, more expensive aluminum
- four-speed transmission, not five speed as in most cars
- one windshield wiper
- tubeless tires
- no radio
- no power-assisted improvements (brakes, doors, windows, steering)

Tata has applied for only 34 patents for the NANO. Consider that GM applies for 280 annually.[3]

The "low cost" strategy is often looked on with disdain because it is seldom a defensible market position. Can the NANO protect its innovation? To answer this question, one must look beyond Tata's manufacturing process, and examine other factors at play.

First, Tata Motors is a subsidiary of Tata Industries, one of the largest conglomerates in India. This invariably gives it purchasing advantages. Through its parent company, Tata has an extensive distribution network that covers not only cars but also 60 percent of the market share in commercial vehicles.[4] Tata also has an extensive network of other businesses through which it is able to gain cost advantages in areas other than manufacturing. As one of the largest, most recognized brands in India, it enjoys the ability to incur lower marketing costs. It has also secured the use of subsidized land, presumably through strong ties with local governments, further lowering costs. And since the Indian automotive market is highly protected, with foreign manufacturers requiring a joint venture partner, competition is limited.

Very few companies in India can compete with Tata, which seems likely to maintain its size and price innovation advantage.

Think differently: Eee PC in Taiwan

Cars are not the only modern products benefiting from price innovations. Computers were once considered out of reach of most people in the developing and newly developed worlds. Indeed the charity OLPC (One Laptop Per Child) was established to provide a basic laptop to children in developing countries so they had the chance to learn and embrace the digital world. Major corporations such as AMD, Brightstar Corporation, eBay, Google, Marvell, News Corporation, SES, Nortel Networks, Red Hat, and Taiwan's Quanta are all participating in the project. (Quanta, for example, developed and produced the laptop.)[5] Countries such as Afghanistan, Cambodia, Haiti, Mexico, Mongolia, Peru, Rwanda, Uruguay, and the US (Birmingham, Alabama) have purchased the laptops for their children.

When the OLPC charity was announced in 2005, laptops were considered expensive. Since then, they have been made affordable not just for charity purposes, but in the marketplace. A key player in this has been the well-established Taiwanese notebook company, Asus. Asus has developed its own simplified, low-cost laptop, the Eee PC. This was launched at the end of 2007 and took the world by surprise because of its price: only $299. This is the first branded laptop to sell for less than even some mobile phones. Because of the significantly lower price, laptop purchases can now seem almost trivial everyday decisions.

Within the first two months of the Eee PC's launch, Asus claimed to have sold more than 300,000 units, greater than the overall 2007 OLPC unit sales. Even though it does not have some features readily available in other products in the market, its record reflects the market attraction of a reduced-feature, low-cost laptop.

The Eee PC has other winning qualities too. It is lightweight, and has a user-friendly interface and a stylish appearance with different trendy colors. This reflects Asus' ambiguous marketing positioning for this new product. The company doesn't want to promote the laptop solely on the basis of its low cost. It also doesn't want to position it as an ultra-mobile PC (UMPC) or even an upgraded level of PDA, and, apparently, does not want comparisons with OLPC. Rather, the Eee is presented as easy to use, with characteristics broadly appealing to women, children, and the elderly.

The Eee PC has been a continuous top seller in the Japanese market since its launch, and has gained some share of the notebook PC market. The results have been far greater than expectations, even within the company. Asus did not create a special internal team to develop the product over the long term, nor did it predict sales demand, which has led to shortages and waiting lists.

The success of the Eee PC says a lot about the PC industry, and Asian players in particular. The product was designed in Taiwan by a former OEM/ODM company that turned itself around to develop its own branded products and sell them to Hong Kong, China, Japan, and the rest of the world. Asus' experience shows that for emerging economies in Asia, the world is changing. They have gained new skill sets and learned quickly, and they can develop products that not only meet basic needs, but have trendy appeal. They have also found they do not need to incorporate all the latest technologies. Rather, they can follow their instincts and achieve success. The Eee PC demonstrates that trendy low-cost products are welcome not only in less-developed countries, but also developed ones, and even among discerning Japanese consumers.

Business innovations in China

In China, business innovations not only are good for the companies involved, but are seen as important factors in the country's future success. China's President Hu Jintao has emphasized the importance of independent innovation in furthering China's growth in its eleventh five-year plan (2006–10).[6]

Encouraging innovation: Internet business in China

Online shopping in China has been slow to develop despite the millions of Internet users there. Shopping in China has traditionally been characterized by face-to-face bargaining, cash on delivery, and lack of confidence in the final product. These factors are still driving the habits of consumers.[7]

And yet, there are signs of change. "Teambuy" (*tuangou*) has become one of the most successful shopping platforms that provide nationwide coverage. It negotiates with retailers or suppliers of popular items for a bulk purchase discount, then organizes buyers to purchase the product at a bargain price at a particular time and place. The revenues come from commissions provided by the suppliers or retailers as well as from advertisements.

The idea of "group purchasing" companies has not taken off in the West—witness the failure of letsbuyit.com during the dotcom boom—but the situation in Asia is different. Deloitte described "mob shopping" as a new trend in online consumer shopping in Asia in its 2008 Industry Outlook.[8]

The idea is an offshoot of the flash mobs and pillow fights[9] that emerged in New York's Central Park, now transformed into an innovative e-commerce consumer-to-business model that taps into China's consumer power. The key to its success is in matching Chinese shopping habits.

Challenges for outsiders: the case of eBay

Meg Whitman, the CEO of eBay, said in 2005 that "market leadership in China will be a defining characteristic of leadership globally."[10] China clearly is a pivotal market for modern multinational firms. When it comes to online opportunities, many companies are active in the China market.

The China online advertisement market was predicted to reach $3.6 billion in 2010, according to research by UBS. Many outsiders believe they can catch the market wave by replicating mature models developed elsewhere in the fully open and borderless Internet world. MySpace, a social networking website with more than 115 million registered users, expects to generate annual revenues of $400–$500 million. However, that may be easier said than done. China's strict censor control filters out "suspected" sensitive information, compromising site usability. This, plus the number of fast-moving copycats in the country, slows the growth not only of MySpace but also other big players such as Facebook and Google.[11] Local players such as Baidu are gaining ground. Armed with better knowledge of the house rules in a planned economy, Baidu has succeeded in capturing a 62 percent share of the search and advertising market.[12]

A classic example of a company that has not managed to capitalize on the growing markets in Asia is eBay. Although eBay introduced innovations in other markets, it has not been as effective in

China, chiefly because it has not adapted its business model. Its experiences with the local competition highlighted the challenges faced by sticking to models developed elsewhere.

One of eBay's competitors was EachNet, founded in 1999 to offer online auction services. EachNet's success made eBay sit up and take notice. In 2002, eBay purchased one-third of EachNet for $30 million, and bought the remainder in 2003 for an additional $150 million to facilitate its penetration of the China market.[13] By 2004, eBay EachNet had more than four million registered users. The company overcame the issue of trust for online auctions by requiring its sellers to submit Chinese identity cards for verification.[14]

At the same time a new challenger emerged. Taobao is a spin-off from Alibaba.com that entered the market much later, in 2003, and by 2004 had exceeded 500,000 registered users. To achieve initial market penetration against the bigger name of eBay, the site charged no commission or trading fees. By the first quarter of 2005, Taobao was already beating eBay EachNet in terms both of "page views per user" (10.7 for Taobao compared to 7.4 for eBay) and gross merchandise value (GMV), where Taobao declared $120 million compared to eBay's $90 million.

By this time, eBay had launched its PayPal payment system in China. However, it was hampered by low levels of trust and low market penetration of credit cards in China. In February 2005, Taobao announced the introduction of Alipay, its direct competitor to PayPal. In the words of CEO Jack Ma, "When it comes to online payment systems, one size does not fit all. There is an American model for America, a European model for Europe, and the Alipay model for China."[15]

Although Taobao and eBay used similar models for ranking the reliability and trustworthiness of buyers and sellers, the issue of trust remained central to the online auction market. Alipay tackled this by taking the role of a trusted third party that allowed the buyer to transfer funds to be held in escrow. Once the buyer receives the goods from the seller, Alipay will release the funds.

It isn't that eBay EachNet didn't try. By the time Alipay was launched, EachNet actually had an escrow system in place: Au Fu Tong. PayPal functionality came later and separately. But Alipay took extra steps to ensure its innovative approach truly dealt with the issue of trust by partnering with four of China's largest banks and providing a cast-iron guarantee against fraud. According to a Morgan Stanley report in 2005, "In our view, Alipay may continue its lead in the domestic payment market because it helps to resolve the settlement risks among buyers and sellers through its escrow mechanism."[16]

By September 2005, the Morgan Stanley report noted that Taobao had 10 times the listings of eBay EachNet. It concluded that the user-friendliness of the Taobao interface, its customer-centricity, and the social network and graphical nature of Taobao were more conducive than the eBay interface to promoting a better user experience and therefore user "stickiness."

eBay was under continuing pressure from the Taobao market share, and by late 2006, it had sold the majority of its operations in China to a local partner, tom.com. While stating that "eBay has helped pioneer e-commerce in China, and by combining our expertise with that of a strong local partner like Tom Online, we are even better positioned to participate in this growing market,"[17] this was effectively an admission of defeat in the China market. After this move, Taobao saw transactions double for 2007 over the previous year, and solidified its dominant position.[18]

The Morgan Stanley paper noted that there were lessons here for foreign Internet companies in China. "We believe the ongoing battle between Alibaba and eBay underscores the key challenges faced by foreign Internet companies in China, and reinforces our view that foreign companies that . . . could better leverage local elements may have better odds for success in China."[19] In other words, if Internet companies want to penetrate new markets, they need to innovate their products to match the needs of the local market, rather than seek to adapt the local market to their international product. Using the innovation agenda and having a better knowledge of Chinese culture will offer a better chance of success in climbing the Chinese Wall.

Competing in opening China

One challenging period faced by local Asian business leaders was when leading international luxury brand operators entered China in large numbers. Asian entrepreneurs, particularly from Hong Kong, had invested early, after Deng Xiaoping opened the country to the outside world. From the 1980s, many Asian brands experienced great success in China, and soon established themselves as leading luxury brands for various consumer products there. However, as the country prospered, international competitors started to move in. Local Asian companies suffered when competing head-on with global players that had more sophisticated business models and marketing tools.

The phenomenal economic growth in China over the past two decades has made the country one of the largest markets for luxury goods. This was further boosted when China joined the WTO, leading to lower tariffs on imported goods. While the Chinese have a strong culture of saving significant portions of their income, research has also suggested that the emerging middle class will continue to increase spending on luxury goods.[20]

Given the prospects of growth and strong long-term outlook, masses of international luxury brands began to enter the China market from the early-1990s, sometimes piggybacking leading regional retailers such as Lane Crawford and Dickson Concepts (which represents such brands as Polo, Brooks Brothers, and DuPont). While most operations were initially unprofitable, these operators saw their initial losses as investments into a market where they knew they would prevail. The arrival of these quality operators in China put significant pressure on Asian brands because the retail ambience, display, presence, and merchandise were generally more sophisticated than those of traditional outlets, leading consumers to question whether Asian brands were really the "top-end" brand they had been led to believe. At the same time, overseas travel restrictions were eased for Chinese residents, so they could spend their money elsewhere. The combination of these factors was a blow to Asian businesses, which saw a steady decline in both revenue and profit.

Asian business leaders have the advantage of being close to the fastest-growing economy—China—and possessing a deeper understanding of Chinese culture and traditions than do those from outside the region. But unless they are willing to evolve, invest, and compete with the best in the world, this inborn advantage won't persist. Chinese consumers are still at the discovery stage, and the expectation of brand loyalty should not be high. A brand should instead find its place in the market where its strengths lie and differentiate itself from the global players. An example of this is appliance maker Haier, which is not a only dominant player in China, but competes in the world market head-on with global players.

Global brand luxury goods have their weaknesses though. The protection of their brand equity is so important that they have a strong tendency to operate their own shops. This puts limitations on the pace of expansion, and provides local brands with a valued advantage: they can provide superior retail coverage over global brands. Local brands should take note.

Protecting your innovations

In the global economy, protecting innovations abroad is critical to advancing competitiveness. It is also important at the national level. Intellectual property protection is critical to every country's economic development, embracing as it does the promotion of indigenous innovations, creativity, and access to innovations by consumers and producers.

The former US trade representative Susan Schwab has indicated that piracy and counterfeiting levels in China remain unacceptably high. In 2007, her office said inadequate protection of intellectual property rights in China cost US firms billions of dollars each year.[21] For some products, it also posed a serious risk of harm to consumers in China, the US, and around the world. Schwab acknowledged that China had taken steps to improve the protection of intellectual property rights, but said, "we have not been able to agree on several important changes to China's legal regime that we believe are required by China's WTO commitments." Her office also claimed that Chinese law created a "safe harbor" for distributors of pirated and counterfeit products because it set thresholds that had to be met before the government would initiate criminal prosecution. Chinese authorities recently have lowered that threshold from 1,000 to 500 pirated copies of a protected work.[22]

There are other signs of a tougher line in China. The US coordinator for international intellectual property enforcement in the Department of Commerce, Chris Israel, has cited several court cases won by rights holders, including a December 2005 case involving fake luxury handbags, in which the Chinese court ordered the owner of Beijing's Silk Street Market—rather than the vendors of the counterfeit goods—to pay damages. "This is an important ruling because the Chinese courts are finally holding landlords responsible for the illegal activities of their tenants," Israel said.[23]

The marketplace in China

The existence of gray and black markets provides a platform for counterfeiters. These markets sell both authentic brand and counterfeit products. The authentic product can be purchased from authorized dealers or imported from overseas, while the counterfeit products are sourced from counterfeit manufacturers. These markets operate on a massive scale. The Silk Market in Beijing and XiangYang Market in Shanghai are two of the most famous such markets in China (although XiangYang Market was demolished in 2007).

The sale of counterfeit goods through the Internet exacerbates the situation. The Internet is easy to access and easy to hide in, and rules and regulations can be hard to enforce on Internet transactions. Most importantly, the Internet attracts a massive audience seven days a week, 24 hours a day, which makes it difficult to police.

Gray and black markets offer benefits to consumers and traders. Consider this:

- For consumers, these markets normally sell counterfeit products at a price lower than that of authentic products, so they get "branded" items at a much cheaper rate.
- For traders, they can earn big profits selling counterfeit products compared with selling the authentic brand. The cost of counterfeit products is significantly lower because they don't have the expense of quality control, design, and so on.
- Traders also benefit from light administrative penalties. Enforcement agents can rarely trace a counterfeit product from the marketplace all the way down the supply chain. Although the manufacture of counterfeit goods is a problem, clamping down on manufacturers is very difficult, especially because local protection may also need to be overcome.
- Counterfeit goods are not the only problem. Authentic products sourced through improper distribution channels also feed into these markets.

Global brands are not sitting on the problem. In 2000, a group of multinational firms established an anti-counterfeiting coalition, the Quality Brands Protection Committee (QBPC). By 2008, it had more than 160 members. The mission of the QBPC is to work cooperatively with the Chinese central and local governments to make positive contributions to intellectual property protection in China.

Prevention measures: strategic and operational actions

To protect technology and business secrets, companies are advised to carefully select which products and technologies they will sell or manufacture in China. They should also take care in selecting appropriate business partners, customers, and staff, and reinforce intellectual property protection awareness by implementing security measures, requiring noncompete clauses, and frequently monitoring the activities of their Chinese business partners to minimize potential leaks, among other things.[24]

They might do well to take a lesson from Firestone Tire & Rubber. When Firestone planned to set up a compensation trade for technology transfer to China several years ago, it chose to sell slightly dated radial tire technology. The technology was not the most current in the US or Japan, but it was appropriate for China, southeast Asia, and Africa. The concept was to sell the same technology several times in China to each of the major tire manufacturers. To prevent buyers from sharing the technology with SOEs and their distributors throughout China, Firestone chose to deal with the biggest tire manufacturers in Shanghai and Guangzhou, assuming that they would be big enough to resist state pressure to disclose company secrets. In addition, the contract gave Firestone the right to terminate buyback if it determined that technology had been leaked to the state or another tire manufacturer. Firestone sold the same technology twice within 12 months, earning US$60 million, and managed to protect the confidentiality of the technology.[25]

Conclusion

Asia presents opportunities and challenges that can differ wildly from those in other markets. While Asian companies are exploiting innovation to differentiate themselves and sustain growth, companies from outside the region need to brush up on their local knowledge and develop local partnerships.[26] Firms such as eBay have business models centered entirely upon innovative ideas that, in their original markets, gained significant market share but in Asia were insufficiently innovative to repeat that success. Failure to adapt business models to the best advantage can result in lost market share and, in the worst case, the need to withdraw from the region altogether.

Lessons can be learned from innovations such as the NANO, Eee PC, Teambuy, and Alipay. They achieved success because they were differentiated from other products in the market, and their design and marketing factored in local elements such as culture, habits, and trust. As a result, the companies behind these products were able to defend their market position against both legal competitors and those who would unfairly seek to undermine their position through intellectual property theft and other illegal means.

RON MCEACHERN, former President, PepsiCo International for Asia

"You can never have enough insight into your customer."

Launching Lays in China sounds like a pretty simple thing to do. Just duplicate the plans. At that point, 10 years ago, Lays was a $3 billion business in North America, the number one salty snack.

One of the first things they tell you is don't worry, the Chinese love to snack. They are in fact some of the biggest macro snackers in the world—the macro snack market in China is worth $10 billion. Only the US and Thailand top them.

But the fact they eat a lot of snacks is not immediately relevant in the least. You talk to them about potato chips, consumer potato chips, salty snacks, and they say, who's supposed to eat it? In the morning or afternoon? Do I eat it for lunch; is it a snack; is it a food? Do I eat it at home; do I eat it while watching TV; can I eat it on the train; can I eat it at the office? It's not immediately intuitive why they even want it.

It's very difficult to change habits. What you have to do is adapt to habits. How do you tell someone who is eating rice crackers, or dried fruit or nuts, or meat or seeds, that they should immediately eat a Lays potato chip?

(continued)

(*continued*)

The more you focus what your marketing activity is going to be, the more precisely you can define your objective and measure, and the more effective you can be. Do you want males, females, at what age?

You go for viable penetration, frequency, and amount. That simple equation throws up a whole lot of marketing thoughts. One is, you really, really need to understand your consumer. Number two is, you need to broaden the appeal.

Potato chips in China are eaten by young women while watching TV in the evening. That's not a very robust target audience. How do you get them to take it on the train, to the office, to the school, to the Internet café? In China, they don't like getting their fingers messy; they don't like making a lot of noise; they don't like eating in the office. You need to set a creative marketing direction.

Frankly, in a market that is not that used to a product like this, you have to tell them why they want to eat it; when they want to eat it; who they want to eat it with. You want to solve the emerging health and welfare issues; you want to manage the innovation process; and you've got to go quickly.

Our research showed 84 percent of Lays consumers were young women, mainly at home, who thought it was modern and trendy. But that's really not important to me. They didn't eat a lot of it because it was low in food content, which triggered a whole bunch of thoughts—how do we innovate the product; how do we innovate the package?

We changed the product. It has a $3 billion pedigree and you don't mess with Frito Lays. We decided we had to change the product, the package, and the advertising in China.

First of all was flavor. Local cuisine has an incredibly powerful connection, relevance and familiarity. So we developed a process called Master Chef. We would get a local Hangzhou chef who was very well known, and get him to mix up Hangzhou stewed beef. Our people attempted to duplicate that and put it on a potato chip. Hangzhou stewed beef, grilled lobster, nori seaweed—these don't play in North America. We continue to look at new breakthroughs like flavor encapsulation, ways of getting multiple top notes on a product.

We also looked at flavor direction. There's a lot of ways you can have grilled, savory, spicy, and sweet. We start getting into

(*continued*)

spicy seafood, spicy meat, aromatic spicy, sweet spicy, numb spicy. We start putting this on a chip, and it has appeal.

Here's another one. We also thought one of the reasons Chinese people didn't like chips is they are seen as heating foods. In China, there are heating foods and cooling foods. Fried foods are heating, so they wouldn't eat them in the summer. So we launched lemon, cherry, and tomato flavored potato chips, cucumber chips.

It had a dramatic impact. Flavor is incredibly important. Older women like cool. So we evolved the flavors to cool and natural, took away MSG and some artificial flavors, changed the graphics, made the chips more natural. Then we ran into problems. We were making them too feminine.

Men, in China, felt snacking was effeminate. We found out that by making a bigger chip, calling it Max, changing the positioning to be more aggressive—now we were evolving it even further. We got into active sports and really intense flavors—the numb spicy flavors. Size matters, like big watches, so we made big chips. We put the intensity of the spice on the chip, making it visible to men. That wouldn't play in New York.

We also asked, why aren't people eating us more frequently? They were mainly eating chips at home. Why wasn't it getting out to the street?

It's considered bad form to eat in the office—it's not fashionable and it makes noise. Surfing the Internet, they get the keyboard all dirty—there's an inappropriateness there.

We decided we needed to get out into these areas even a little bit further. We bought a company that can create canisters, and put a thing called a dragon boat in it. It's a little plastic sleeve that holds the chips. We had found that Chinese women would often eat potato chips with Kleenex. The tray is elegant and formal, can be hidden in the office, and has had incredible success: it's easy to share, it's so tasty. Now we have blown away Pringles. Imitation is the sincerest form of flattery, and everyone else is coming out with trays.

We fundamentally changed the flavor of the chip, fundamentally changed the package design, and changed Lays' position.

If you are in the consumer market, you can never have enough insight into your consumer. You can never found your plans solidly enough on insights.

(continued)

(continued)

The reason Pepsi is the number one softdrink in China is that Chinese consumers think Pepsi is a Chinese brand. If you can do that type of retail, it's only the ego in New York that gets bruised.

MARJORIE YANG, Chair of Esquel Group

"We make what other people cannot make ... That's our whole niche."

We are not just a manufacturer. We're actually a service provider and that completely changes the requirements. People say, vertically integrated—is that stupid? You're better off to outsource things you are not good at. You can get better quality; it's cheaper; and you can get more variety and flexibility.

The reason we got into cotton was very simple. We need upland cotton—very thin, very fine, longer, stable cotton. Only a few places in the world produce this, and Xinjiang happens to be one of them.

The Chinese government has made cotton a government-controlled commodity, and incentivizes farmers to crossbreed upland cotton with other types. The farmers are not stupid; they get a higher income from the higher yields. That's why we had to jump in, because otherwise we would be losing that length in the cotton.

I had no intention of being a cotton farmer. Anything that's a commodity, you just buy it. But we were getting more and more focused on controlling the quality.

We do our own ginning, and we teach the farmers to separate their cotton from the chickens and ducks. Farmers take the cotton home and don't store it separately, but we taught them to do that and we pay a premium. Otherwise, we have to pick up the foreign matter downstream, and that's very expensive.

That's how we got better control of quality.

We made a conscious effort to specialize. We are in a niche market. We make what other people cannot make or won't make. That's our whole niche; that's our whole theory for staying alive. What other people don't want to do or cannot do, then we do.

Notes

1 Innovaro "Innovaro Briefing 10-05: Innovation in Asia," n.d. http://www.inno varo. com/inno_updates/Innovation%20Briefing%2010-05.pdf.

2 IPR, "Singapore: Recommendations to Foster Innovation and Competitiveness," IPR Strategic Business Information Database, June 25, 2007.

3 Yahoo! Finance Singapore, "Learning from Tata's Nano," February 28, 2008. http://sg.biz.yahoo.com/080228/68/4exk5.html.

4 Keith Naughton, "Small. It's the New Big," *Newsweek*, February 25, 2008.

5 Quanta, "About Quanta Computer," http://www.quantatw.com/Quanta/ english/product/qci_olpc.aspx.

6 *China Daily*, "President Hu Delivers New Year Address," January 1, 2006. http://www.chinadaily.com.cn/english/doc/2006-01/01/content_508487.htm.

7 Simon Montlake, "China's New Shopping Craze: Team Buying," *Christian Science Monitor*, December 5, 2007. http://articles.moneycentral.msn.com/Savingand Debt/FindDealsOnline/ChinasNewShoppingCrazeTeamBuying.aspx.

8 Deloitte, "2008 Cross Industry Outlook," 2008. http://www.deloitte.com/dtt/ cda/doc/content/us_2008CrossIndustryOutlook20080111.pdf.

9 See Mobile Clubbing website, http://www.mobile-clubbing.com.

10 Jeffrey Ressner, "Why ebay Must Win China," *Time*, August 22, 2005. http://www.time.com/time/magazine/article/0,9171,1096486-1,00.html.

11 Bambi Francisco, "My-censored-Space in China," *Marketwatch*, December 5, 2006. http://www.marketwatch.com/news/story/myspace-faces-many-challenges-china/story.aspx?guid={3DFC31EE-39B6-4156-A6B0-0DDD93B4AF4F}.

12 *The Standard*, "Hunt for Profits," April 30, 2007. http://finance.thestandard .com.hk/chi/money_news_view.asp?aid=43284.

13 Ressner, ibid.

14 Mary Meeker, Lina Choi, and Yoshiko Motoyama, "The China Internet Report," Morgan Stanley, April 14, 2004. http://www.morganstanley.com/institutional/ techresearch/pdfs/China_Internet_Report0404.pdf.

15 Alibaba.com, "Alibaba.com Launches Online Payment Solution in China," February 2, 2005. http://resources.alibaba.com/article/348/Alibaba_com_ launches_online_payment_solution_in_China.htm.

16 Richard Ji and Mary Meeker, "China Internet: Creating Consumer Value in Digital China," Morgan Stanley, September 12, 2005. http://www.morganstanley .com/institutional/techresearch/China_Internet_091205.html?page=research.

17 *China Tech News*, "eBay Partners with Tom.com in Chinese Auction Website Deal," December 20, 2006. http://www.chinatechnews.com/2006/12/20/4759-ebay-still-thinks-it-can-win-in-china/.

18 Sophie Taylor, "China Auction Site Taobao Saw Transactions Double in 2007," *Reuters*, January 21, 2008. http://www.reuters.com/article/rbssTech Media TelecomNews/idUSSHA3336820080122.

19 Ji and Meeker, ibid.

20 *McKinsey Quarterly*, special edition,"The Value of China's Emerging Middle Class," 2006.

21 America.gov, "United States Calls for Trade Consultations with China," April 9, 2007. http://www.america.gov/st/business-english/2007/April/2007 040 9171956zjsredna0.7277948.html.

22 ibid.

23 America.gov, "Intellectual Property Rights Protection Weak in China, US Says," June 7, 2006. http://www.america.gov/st/washfile-english/2006/June/200606 08164932cagnoud0.1814234.html.

24 Meagan C. Dietz, Sharena Shao-Tin Lin, and Lei Yang, "Protecting Intellectual Property in China," *McKinsey Quarterly*, August, 2005.

25 Dr. Lawrence C. Franklin, Hong Kong University of Science and Technology course material for Business Strategies in Asia Pacific: "Caselet: Firestone Compensation Trade," December, 2007.

26 Innovaro, op. cit.

Chapter 6

The Changing Landscape of Corporate Governance

Corporate governance has become a top priority for market regulators across Asia in recent years, supported by extensive new regulations in most markets, which have brought rapid improvements in key regional countries. However, it is worrying to note a pervasive lack of true corporate governance here, evidenced by a continued slate of company investigations being pursued. Clearly, the financial and wider market benefits to be gained from good governance have yet to be fully appreciated by companies in Asia, with such regulatory requirements being managed as a process exercise, rather than a cultural shift.

The introduction of global governance standards and related company codes started to affect Asia from 1998, after the regionwide financial crisis. More recently, there has been a far more robust phase of implementation, after moves in the US and Europe that were driven by many well-publicized corporate and financial failures, and the implementation of the US Sarbanes-Oxley Act in 2002.

Much progress has been made in lawmaking and regulatory enactments, but the going has been slow when it comes to actual implementation and enforcement. Korea, Japan, and China have had several corporate governance cases in which the final enforcement has fallen short or political interference has affected rulings. Conversely, extremely vigorous cases have been undertaken against companies in some countries that suggest bias, conflicts of interest and political influence (such as Livedoor in 2006). This all points to the need for a more rigorous and process-based Asian governance infrastructure.

There are risks of a two-tier regional class evolving though. The northeast Asian trio of Japan, Korea, and Taiwan are driving steady legal reforms and enforcement actions, as they now acknowledge the tremendous risks to domestic economies of not doing so. Legal loopholes and links between politics and business still pose considerable obstacles in these countries, but the evidence of progress is considerable. The ASEAN nations of southeast Asia, on the other hand, with the exception of Singapore, have much more work to do. Thailand may become another exception because a respectable legal environment was being nurtured until recently.

Another regional risk comes through the recent tendency to focus on corporate enforcement while assuming the legal regulatory work is done. Both aspects of governance control are necessary and require continued active management.

Transparency

Corporate governance ensures that companies are, and continue to be, good stewards of the money invested by shareholders or other investors. Transparency is critical. In corporate governance terms, it can be best described as the disclosure of a company's financial statements, corporate objectives, and internal processes and controls. As eminent economist Bill Witherell said:

> Financial asset pricing requires not only disclosure of accurate financial statements but also disclosure of main corporate objectives, standards and practices. Conveying this information to the market, is, in my view, an essential aspect of transparency . . . the OECD *Principles of Corporate Governance* call for regular, timely and accurate disclosure not only of operating and financial results but also of information on commercial objectives, ownership

structures, boards of directors and key executives and their remuneration, related party transactions, governance structures and
internal controls.[1]

Capital markets and capitalism in general are based on the
concept of investors pricing goods and services based on the risk/
return ratio. The greater the confidence the market has in the results
and other information issued by a company, the greater the market will
value that information, and, thus, the greater the value it will give to
the firm. As Witherell also noted:

> [T]he effectiveness of market discipline is influenced by the
> efficiency of financial markets and that transparency is, in turn,
> a key determinant of market efficiency and the evolution of
> corporate governance . . .
>
> The importance of sound corporate governance to market stability
> and confidence has been dramatically illustrated by a series of
> incidents in the markets of the most advanced economies. These
> revealed certain weaknesses in corporate governance and related
> aspects of the foundations of our markets.[2]

Every firm, be it public or private, is valued by the market, and it is
the goal of those investing in and running a company to see its value
increase. Alan Greenspan summed it up this way: "Corporate managers ideally should be working on behalf of shareholders to allocate
business resources to their optimum use."[3]

Given that transparency is naturally linked to the valuation of a
firm and is a lynchpin of corporate governance, firms should pay
careful attention to their related policies, procedures, and corporate
culture. That requires commitment from the top and a broader
understanding within the whole company. Responsibility must
reach down into the middle management ranks. Pricewaterhouse-
Coopers, in a report with the Economist Intelligence Unit, under-
lined that fact:

> The process of instilling a culture of compliance throughout the
> organization is more important. Good compliance, risk manage-
> ment and governance is the job of every employee, not a few . . .
> What is needed is a new and integrated approach that does not

limit its ambitions to staying out of trouble but strives to improve the quality of an institution's management.[4]

Most companies rely far too much on a legalistic approach, which seeks merely to focus the efforts of employees on compliance with the letter of the laws and regulations in each country. However, this approach does not embrace the breadth and depth of the required disclosures or spirit of transparency that is needed to secure the trust and confidence of the market. As Greenspan said: "Rules cannot substitute for character."[5]

Harvey Pitt, the former head of the Securities and Exchange Commission in the US, has argued that a company should take a holistic approach to transparency by developing a process that goes beyond what regulations and laws stipulate, so that policies include information that will further build investor confidence. Directors, he said, need to be aware of the following:

- The tone is set at the top. Integrity and transparency only become established at lower levels when they exist at the highest level.
- Trust can only exist if companies have internal procedures that can prove the reliability of their numbers.
- Establishing trust and confidence is an ongoing process that involves setting clear responsibility for corporate data.
- Transparency is key. Ask what you would want to know if you were a stockholder.[6]

Building trust in the marketplace can increase the value of a firm. An established reputation for being credible and reliable and living up to the numbers and information provided to the market has other benefits too. With a strong market reputation, the cost of borrowing money and retaining employees is often lower, while the ability to find and hire top-quality employees increases. As Pitt said:

> Investors must be confident a company has told them everything they need to know to make an accurate assessment of the company's current performance and future prospects . . . Effective corporate governance only exists if corporate constituencies can trust what companies say about their financial performance . . . Such policies also increase the likelihood of attracting capital, partners, and the best CEOs.[7]

There is also evidence that a strong corporate governance and transparency program leads to strong financial returns. PricewaterhouseCoopers' view is that "a reputation for integrity is a source of competitive advantage."[8] While Bill Witherell believes: "companies with good corporate governance arrangements in Asia, especially Korea, for example, weathered the financial crisis better than those with less developed governance structures in place."[9]

The ultimate goal of every company is to increase its market value and create wealth for its investors. To that end, it cannot ignore the issue of transparency, which is a critical component of corporate governance, and has a direct link to the value assigned to the firm by the market. Each firm needs to consider its reputation, and to ensure that its corporate governance program has a robust and well-thought-out transparency policy. PricewaterhouseCoopers again:

> The challenge for management is to determine how much un-certainty it is prepared to accept as it strives to grow stakeholder value. Too much uncontrolled risk and a company jeopardizes its own future and its shareholders' capital too; too little and it risks letting the business stagnate . . . It is then up to the board as a whole to monitor that risk and to decide whether the level of risk is compatible with the company's business.[10]

Board of directors

The board of directors has a key role to play in corporate governance. As the representatives of shareholders, they oversee the organization and ensure that its continuous operation is in the best interests of stakeholders. Given the complexity of today's organizations, this is not a simple task.

The primary roles of the board are hiring and firing the CEO, planning for his or her succession, and overseeing the strategy set by management. Boards should also have the following roles and responsibilities:

- board leadership and composition;
- senior executive compensation issues;
- ensuring the quality of the enterprise's products and services;
- performance and financial viability;
- risk management, controls, and transparency;

- setting the tone at the top for ethics and compliance;
- stakeholder issues, including business sustainability in light of climate, energy, environmental, and other concerns.

Most importantly, boards of directors owe a debt of loyalty. When and if conflict exists, "shareholders win," as Dean Emeritus Donald Jacobs told his Kellogg Executive MBA students. Boards also owe a duty of care. Board members must act in good faith, on an informed basis, to inquire and to question. They should honestly believe that an action is in the best interests of the company and its shareholders, although noting that they are protected by the business judgment rule.

Since the board must work closely with management and its CEO, a few dilemmas need to be tackled. First is the issue of independence, a major requirement of an effective board directorship. Any director must be clearly independent of the CEO and management team. Second, while a director must work toward what is best for all shareholders, what then is the tradeoff for the entire company?

This question should go back to the concept of "shareholders win." In other words, all board director decisions must meet the objective of what is best for the shareholders.

Given these requirements, who should serve on boards? The structure of board memberships can vary widely. Membership can be based on whether they are inside or outside, a major customer or supplier, experienced in business or by functional knowledge, a large shareholder, or a serving or retired CEO. It can also be determined by gender, age, race, or actions taken in governance activities and other areas.

Good directors should possess certain attributes or qualities, including:

- understanding the business and having good common sense judgment;
- being skeptical, diligent, and willing to ask basic and tough questions;
- ensuring that answers received from management or the executive directors are understandable to themselves and the full board;
- being vigilant in following through on problems of compliance, audit, and controls;
- most importantly, having the judgment to know when to pursue an issue, rather than simply "going along" to avoid being unpopular.[11]

In directing and monitoring enterprise-related strategies, the board looks closely at the key drivers of performance, and diligently monitors how well they are being applied. The board needs to make sure those drivers are a fundamental part of the business—and to ensure that management is responsible for them. They must create better tools to monitor and measure performance, and set specific performance targets, both financial and nonfinancial.[12] However, these tasks are not always easy to accomplish.

In 2004, Deloitte Touche Tohmatsu, in cooperation with the *Economist* Intelligence Unit, examined key nonfinancial metrics in a report titled "In the Dark: What boards and executives don't know about the health of their businesses." It concluded: "While the over-whelming majority of board members and senior executives say they need incisive non-financial information on their companies' key drivers of success, they largely find such data to be lacking or, when available, of mediocre to poor value."[13]

Almost three years later, Deloitte and the *Economist* Intelligence Unit again worked together to see whether things had changed. Their updated 2007 survey found many board members and senior executives still in the dark about the overall health of their organizations and still lacking high-quality nonfinancial data that they could act upon.[14] "Customer satisfaction, operation performances, innovation and employee commitment" were identified "as key drivers of non-financial performance" targets.[15]

Boards of directors have a means of sending clear signals to their management team, and must now clearly tie executive compensation to the key success factors indicated, both in terms of financial and nonfinancial results.

TSMC (Taiwan Semiconductor Manufacturing Co. Ltd.) offers an example of how a board of directors can provide positive direction for a company. TSMC is the world's largest dedicated semiconductor foundry with revenues representing some 50 percent of the global total within the semiconductor industry. The company has announced on its website: "We believe that the basis for successful corporate governance is a sound and effective board of directors."[16]

TSMC's board consists of eight distinguished members. Their outstanding careers and breadth of experience encompass high technology, finance, business, and management. Four are independent directors: Sir Peter L. Bonfield, former CEO of British Telecommunications; Mr. Thomas J. Engibous, former Chairman, President and CEO of Texas Instruments; Stan Shih, former Chairman of Acer Group; and Carleton (Carly) S. Fiorina, former Chairman and CEO of Hewlett-Packard Co.[17] In 2002, the board established an audit committee and in 2003 a compensation committee. Two years later, in 2005, TSMC received awards in recognition of its corporate governance practices, including the Best Corporate Governance award from *IR Magazine* for the Hong Kong and Taiwan regions and the Best Corporate Governance award from FinanceAsia for the Taiwan region.[18]

Morris Chang, CEO of TSMC, told the well-known Taiwanese publication *Global Views Monthly* that:[19]

> Above all, a corporation's core values must conform to the world-class corporations' core values. They are, 1) Truth with no lies; 2) No easy commitments—once committed, the corporation must defy all difficulties and dangers; 3) Compliance; 4) No corruption or bribery; 5) Undertake social responsibilities; 6) No reliance on political or business relations; 7) Excellent corporate governance.[20]

By contrast, when a board is not clearly aware of the activities of its management team or the true financial state of the corporation, then corporate governance is at grave risk. In Asia, traditional behavior by company boards has been to respect the opinions and judgment of their executive managers at all times, especially when those managers have performed well in the past. This creates great risk when the management's judgment is flawed, even when appearing legitimate. As such, Asian companies remain challenged by such cultural practices and norms, by the pressures to ensure consensus and not rock the boat.

In conclusion, the board of directors performs the vital role of overseeing management to ensure the enterprise benefits shareholders. It holds ultimate responsibility. When and if the board functions effectively and efficiently, then "corporate governance" can achieve its maximum benefit.

Family ownership

When we talk about family ownership or a family business, it is obvious that the company is owned or controlled, and most likely managed, by family members. For many people, the first thing that comes to mind might be a small, unsophisticated operation undertaken by a husband and wife with their children or a few employees. Yes, there are a lot of small businesses like this, but there are also many conglomerates around the world that are family owned.

For example, in the US 20 percent of the top 1,000 firms and one-third of the S&P 500 firms, such as Wal-Mart, Ford, and the *New York Times*, are family owned. In Hong Kong, 15 family groups represent 84 percent of GDP. In Korea, 10 family groups (*chaebols*) control 60 percent of GDP. In Sweden, the Wallenbergs control 55 percent of market capitalization. In India, 20 groups (controlled by 16 families) own 66 percent of private-sector assets. In Germany and China, family groups represent more than 66 percent of GDP and 75 percent of the workforce.[21]

Family ownership, then, means much more than small setups. When it comes to corporate governance, it can be very complicated and common standards, such as the Sarbanes-Oxley Act, may not necessarily be appropriate.

What are the basic values of a family? Love, trust, and care would probably be the most common words used. When a child makes a mistake, parents normally hold a forgiving attitude; there is always a second chance. Harmony and a commitment to long-term relationships will apply. When there is a dispute between family members, the eldest in the family usually has the final say in ending the dispute. Corporate governance in family-owned firms, then, can be quite fragile.

Take the example of one of the richest families in Hong Kong, the Kwok family. The three Kwok brothers control Sun Hung Kai Properties (SHKP), one of the largest publicly listed companies in Hong Kong. The chairman and chief executive was until recently the eldest brother, Walter Kwok Ping-Sheung. In early 2008, Walter Kwok unexpectedly announced through a PR company that he would take a temporary leave of absence. The move triggered speculation over a dispute within the family. Although the company has a total of 17 directors (seven executive directors, six nonexecutive directors, and four independent nonexecutive directors[22]), the stock price fell slightly on rumors that Walter would start up a "new" SHKP on his own because of family squabbles.

A co-founder and nonexecutive director of SHKP and the second-richest man in Hong Kong, Lee Shau-Kee, gave an insider's view of the situation in a media interview. "Yes, there was a small conflict between the three brothers, but their mother stopped the dispute by making Walter step aside for a moment. Don't worry, my partner [the late father of the Kwok brothers] was smart enough to put their SHKP shares under a trust fund; none of the brothers can separate the shares. It is impossible for Walter to start up any new SHKP."[23] From this incident, we can see that even though SHKP is well established and its stock normally performs better than Hong Kong's Hang Seng Index, and even though its corporate governance is supposedly perceived as strong and healthy, when it comes to family conflicts, things are handled differently. The chairman has to step aside on his mother's say-so to avoid further conflict within the family. Was this decision the best for the company and for all the shareholders and stakeholders? We don't yet know, but it was certainly good for the Kwok family.

Another example of a family-owned business is Crown World-wide Group of Companies (Crown Group), although there is a completely different kind of corporate governance here. Crown Group is wholly owned by James Thompson. Thompson is in his late 60s and a very successful and typical entrepreneur. He started his company in 1965 with US$500 in savings, and now Crown Group has more than 4,000 full-time staff and is the largest privately owned company in the field of international removals, with operations in more than 200 locations in 50 countries.[24] Thompson has two children, a son and a daughter, who work in senior management within the group; at the top executive board level, there are only three people, Thompson, who is chairman and chief executive, and two other executives who have worked for him for more than 20 years. In discussion with the authors of this chapter, he said there was no independent director in his company although, after 40 years in business, he had recently been thinking about this issue. Thompson makes all the decisions for the company. He is like a king and this is his empire. Corporate govern-ance for Thompson is not on the books but in his mind.

These two examples show that family-owned companies can be very successful. The general attitude of such companies toward corporate governance is that it is more of a family or personal issue, rather than a duty owed to the shareholders or stakeholders. They seem to have nothing to do with the common standard of corporate governance, the Sarbanes-Oxley Act, and instead have their own workable logic on the issue.

Investors or shareholders in family-controlled companies could ask for Sarbanes-Oxley Act-like corporate governance to protect their interests. However, the Sarbanes-Oxley Act standard is built upon a structure quite different from family-owned businesses. It requires the separation of the board and senior management, a transparent process and ultimate accountability by the senior management. The board of directors and independent directors can challenge the management decisions if needed. This is exactly the opposite approach of family-owned businesses.

Family businesses look for harmonious and supportive relationships among family members, and family members are board members as well as part of the management team. In many cases, major business decisions can be made before the official board meeting, as in the SHKP example. Once senior family members make an important decision, they want to keep that information within the family. Other family members will seldom criticize the decision openly, to show their respect and support.

If we insist on Sarbanes-Oxley Act-like standards in a traditional family business, it may destroy the harmony of the family and kill the business. On the other hand, are we going to allow the family members to act on their own wishes, as long as it is within the legal boundary? In addition, as the third and fourth generations come along, the business can involve not only father and sons and brothers and sisters, but also uncles and cousins. The whole structure of the family business could become very complicated. As an investor, how can we monitor the business and the family's performance? What can we do to protect shareholders' interests without harming the business? The solution is quite clear: we need to consider different types of corporate governance.

The most common corporate governance model is the market model. It is found in large and mature markets, such as New York and London, and used by companies such as General Electric, Sony, and HSBC. It has four characteristics:

- large and dispersed ownership with short-term performance objectives to the benefit of the shareholders;
- separation of management and ownership based on the agency theory;
- the board plays a monitoring role;
- the board consists of mostly independent directors.[25]

But there is also another form of corporate governance, the control model, which fits better with family ownership and has somewhat different characteristics:

- concentrated ownership with long-term objectives for the company and all stakeholders, including nonmanagement family members, for sustainability and the preservation of family values;
- often lacking separation of ownership from management;
- key selection criteria being accountability and objectivity rather than independence;
- input from family is essential;
- filling skill gap.[26]

Some examples of the control model include Fiat SA, Italy; Samsung, Korea; and SHKP in Hong Kong. As mentioned, all three brothers of the Kwok family, as well as some of their children and relatives, hold senior positions, including chairman, vice chairman, and managing director, and are involved in the company's daily operations.

Some family-owned businesses in Hong Kong, such as Li & Fung and Eu Yan Sang International Ltd., are more than 100 years old, and are managed by the third or fourth generations. Interestingly, William Fung, group managing director of Li & Fung, originally had no intention to work for the family business, but his father had health problems and asked him to help out. Richard Eu, Chairman of Eu Yan Sang, has said his father didn't want him to get involved in the family business because of the huge conflicts among family members at the time, but Richard insisted.[27] Both are now able to keep their family values and traditions intact, while running their businesses very well. They have invited independent directors to their boards and increased transparency to their shareholders. Both believe their companies can be managed by professional managers instead of family members. They have no problem staying away from daily operations, instead fulfilling their roles as the major shareholders and members of their boards.

We know that family-owned companies can be very successful because of their unity, reduced conflict, better communication between management and the board, and business strategies that don't only focus on short-term results (sometimes they plan for the next generation). There are many forms of corporate governance for family ownership, from a king-like style, which involves controlling every detail, to a majority shareholding position, which stays away from daily operations, and anywhere in between. Family members can play a very flexible role regarding the board and management. They can work on either side or both sides of the structure, depending on their personal interests and capabilities.

To improve corporate governance in family-owned businesses though, the board should consider:

- having more members;
- minimizing personal bias;
- introducing independent directors and nonfamily members onto the board;
- making sure there is enough expertise and variety of opinion before making any major business decisions.

The board should set company strategies, goals and milestones for the management. Management should be hired based on their skills and credentials. If family members are capable, they can fill the job; if not, professional managers should be brought in to run the company.

Most importantly, the board must hold the management accountable for each job. This is not like the monitoring style under the market model, in which the management is penalized for any misbehavior. Mentoring is one of the key functions of the family board. From time to time, the board has to make sure that management does not deviate much from the "master" plan, and it must provide guidance. Corporate governance in family ownership is all about mentoring and accountability. The balance of power and maintenance of good relations among the board, management, and company as a whole, is sometimes even more crucial than short-term profits in these businesses.

Listing requirements

To understand the whys and wherefores of listing requirements, it helps to go back to the Great Crash of 1929 in the US. Before then, there was little support for federal regulation of the securities market. Tempted by the promises of "rags to riches" transformations and easy credit, most investors gave little thought to the danger inherent in uncontrolled market operation. It is estimated that of the $50 billion in new securities offered during the 1920s, half became worthless.

After the Great Crash, public confidence in the market plummeted. There was a consensus that for the economy to recover, the public's faith in the capital market needed to be restored. The US Congress held hearings to identify the problems and search for solutions. Based on the findings in these hearings, Congress passed the *Securities Act 1933* and the *Securities Exchange Act 1934*. As stated in section 2 of the Securities Exchange Act, transactions in securities "are affected with a national interest which makes it necessary to provide for regulation and control of such transactions and of practices and matters relating thereto."

The laws were designed to restore investor confidence in the capital market by providing more structure and government oversight. Congress also established the SEC in 1934 to enforce the securities laws, to promote stability in the market and to protect investors. The two acts continue to provide the basis for the regulation of the securities market today.

Hong Kong has followed a similar path, albeit much later. Until the mid-1970s, stock and commodities markets in Hong Kong were largely unregulated. After the stockmarket crash of 1973–74, the government intervened and enacted core legislation governing the securities and futures industry to restore investor confidence.

To examine why regulation is needed, it helps to look at what it sets out to do. Generally, regulations aim to protect investors and ensure market confidence by minimizing the chances of repeated market disruption and chaos. Investor protection is also a critical criteria for the development and success of the finance industry. For example, the US *Securities Act 1933* has two basic objectives:

- ensuring that investors receive financial and other significant information concerning securities being offered for public sale;
- prohibiting deceit, misrepresentations and other frauds in the sale of securities.

Consider, also, the International Organization of Securities Commissions, which aims to protect investors; ensure fair, efficient and transparent markets; and reduce systemic risk. Or the UK *Financial*

Services & Markets Act 2000, which sets out objectives to promote market confidence, promote public awareness, protect consumers and reduce financial crime.

In Hong Kong, the Security and Futures Commission's (SFC) objectives are to:

- maintain and promote the fairness, efficiency, competitiveness, transparency, and orderliness of the securities and futures industry;
- promote public understanding of the operation and functioning of the industry;
- provide protection for members of the public investing in or holding financial products;
- minimize crime and misconduct in the industry;
- reduce systemic risks in the industry;
- assist the Financial Secretary in maintaining the financial stability of Hong Kong by taking appropriate steps in relation to the industry.

As presented, regulations are intended to protect investors and ensure market confidence by minimizing the chances of repeated market disruption and chaos. Investor protection is also a critical criterion for the development and success of the finance industry.

Regulations are not static, however. They evolve for many reasons, whether it be in securities, banking, insurance, or something as unrelated as intercollegiate athletics. Advances in technology may prompt new stock trading rules. International accords may require new accounting standards. In other cases, regulatory changes are a response to problems that have surfaced. Following is a brief discussion of the major forces driving change.

Technology

Market growth is so fast and bewildering that people have struggled to understand its implications. Basically all financial markets are networks. In the early years of the twenty-first century, these networks have become enormous because they have the technological means to extend their reach around the world. Metcalfe's Law says that the value of a network is exponentially related to the number of its users.

So the wider the network of users, the more valuable is the network and its network externalities. This explains why banking networks are converging horizontally and vertically, linking and merging with securities networks, insurance networks, and even consumer networks. Networks are public utilities, which create a public good. But the minute disparate networks are linked together, their problems are your problems and your problems are theirs. So network economics and network externality effectively drive globalization, which is the linking of local networks to form global networks. It has driven online trading, which has created 24/7 (24 hours a day, seven days a week) transactions. Consequently, markets don't sleep, so regulators can't sleep. In other words, technology and globalization have changed the whole market structure and also the nature of competition.

Globalization

The jurisdictional lines have been blurred by globalization, both within markets and across borders. Where does an electronic transaction stop when an Australian trades Brazilian bonds through a Hong Kong broker who clears the transaction through New York? Property rights are being exchanged across different time zones and different geographical boundaries, cutting across the jurisdictions of banking and securities regulators.

We have global markets, but our laws and regulations are all local. So how do we protect investors' property rights when there are no global laws?

Competition

Amid these technological and global changes, competition has become very intense. The range of new financial products that is emerging is bewildering, and new players, such as hedge funds, are changing the way we look at markets. Who would have expected that in the first half of 2007, one-quarter of Hong Kong's savings would go to capital-guaranteed products with derivative features? These products were offered by banks that are now launching hedge funds of their own to compete with brokers and asset managers.

Indeed, hedge funds are new financial animals that are neither homogenous nor aptly described. Many of them don't even hedge. They simply use very different, complex derivative tools and investment strategies. Many of them operate from offshore financial centers, and they are not properly supervised. In some markets, they account for as much as one-quarter of market liquidity.

Restructuring

As we all know, when financial innovation and competition arrive, some people gain while others lose. The financial sector must undergo restructuring. Domestic banks face foreign competition, while smaller financial institutions cannot compete against larger institutions. Old franchises are eroded, so losses begin to accumulate in the financial sector. These losses appear in the form of either nonperforming loans or intermediary failure. Of course, intermediary failure is not simply caused by excessive competition or bad management. Real sector shocks also cause weaker financial institutions to fail. But the fact that intermediaries fail under regulators' watch means that regulators can never escape part of the blame.

However, as can be seen in the following, most of the reforms or significant changes made to listing rules and regulations have been triggered by major market scandals. After a dramatic business failure or a series of unexpected events that reveal vulnerabilities in the existing system, the government, the public and the industry itself push for change.

One of the clearest examples is cited in the introduction to this section: the market crash of 1929[28] and the Great Depression that followed. Federal legislators laid down laws that are the basis for the current system regulating US investment markets. That system has continued to evolve as the industry has grown. In reaction to the market corrections of 1987 and 2000, regulators made major changes designed to prevent a particular chain of events from recurring.

For example, after the 1987 market losses the New York Stock Exchange (NYSE) instituted shutdown mechanisms called circuit breakers[29] to prevent potentially rapid selloffs. When the air came out of the technology bubble in 2000, federal regulators focused on restricting investment analysts who hyped securities issued by their firms' banking clients.

Accounting standards

Since the Asian crisis, we have a much better understanding of the nature of financial sector problems but we do not necessarily have good answers. We do know we should raise accounting standards and bring regulatory standards toward global standards. Given increased risks, we understand the need to increase surveillance, share information, and make contingency plans. However, the environment is changing far too rapidly for meaningful change because of the four major trends cited: technology, globalization, competition, and restructuring.

Disclosure and conflict of interest rules

In 2003, the NYSE faced a crisis like few it had ever known. The NYSE governance structure was perceived to have broken down, its specialist firms were accused of self-dealing at the expense of customers, and public confidence in the NYSE reached historic lows. The NYSE, critics argued, could not effectively manage the conflicts of interest inherent in its structure. In swift response, the NYSE, with SEC approval, implemented sweeping changes to its governance structure. Among other things, the NYSE created a structure in which members of the board of directors were independent of the interests of the NYSE members whom they regulated. The new structure separated market operations from regulation, assured the independence of regulatory decision making, and installed a chief regulatory officer to report directly to the board of directors through the board's regulatory oversight committee. The NYSE also separated the functions of CEO and chair of the board, installed new board members, including a new chair, and hired a new CEO.

Similarly, in 2004 the Stock Exchange of Hong Kong (SEHK) announced amendments to its main board and growth enterprise market listing rules relating to corporate governance issues. It also made changes to the main board rules on initial listing criteria and continuing listing obligations, in response to the incidents in the US. The amendments considered the independence requirements for, and the role and responsibilities of, sponsors, post-listing advisers (to be known as compliance advisers), and IFAs, as well as those of issuers helping sponsors and compliance advisers. The amendments became effective in 2005.

On top of forced changes in response to market scandals, some changes are introduced under less trying circumstances. They may be actively pursued by the investor public, or the regulator itself may want to perfect the protection to investors or adopt new products. In 2003, for example, the SEHK amended the main board listing rules for authorized collective investment schemes (CISs) to: (1) create a listing and trading platform for all CISs authorized by the Securities and Futures Commission (SFC); (2) clarify the respective regulatory roles of the SFC and the SEHK, with the SFC authorizing and monitoring CISs and the SEHK overseeing the CIS's compliance with the listing rules; and (3) streamline the listing process. The amendment provides for the listing of real estate investment trusts.

Backdoor listings have also been targeted over the years. This is the injection of new assets or business into a dormant "shell" company when it is taken over by a new company. This practice can bypass the regulations and requirements for IPOs and be a shortcut to listing status. Backdoor listings also avoid the problem of differences in accounting systems, for instance by normal direct listing of China enterprises or China business (for example, by "H" shares). Time saved from the approval process can allow the purchaser to inject new assets into the shell. To protect investors in such circumstances, the SEHK took steps in 1989 and 1993 to curtail this type of activity. All backdoor listings must be approved by the SEHK and the SFC. The SEHK has the right to treat an acquisition and the injecting of new assets as a new listing if the business nature changes significantly after the transaction.

That system has potential problems, though, related to back-end enforcement under a three-tier regulatory system of self-regulation by front-line market operators, market regulation by the SFC, and government supervision. The new Securities and Futures Ordinance, introduced in 2003, tries to overcome this. It contains the Securities and Futures (Stock Market Listing) Rules that impose a new dual-filing requirement on listing applicants and listed issuers, in which the same information for initial public offerings and ongoing corporate disclosure have to be filed with both the SEHK and the SFC. If the SFC has reason to believe the listing documents or other public announcements or publications contain false or misleading information, then it can direct the SEHK to suspend dealings in the securities of that listed company. To facilitate compliance, the applicant can authorize the SEHK to file materials with the SFC on its behalf.

* * *

The examples described are undoubtedly just the tip of the iceberg. Many changes and reforms have been and will be undertaken in response to market conditions, new technological advances, and globalization. However, while the development of a listing regulatory system is an ongoing process in which no pause can be made, progress can sometimes seem slow. Any changes to regulations can have widespread impacts and that usually requires a long and time-consuming process of consultation.

Nonexecutive directors

The nonexecutive independent directors of a company are outsiders. They do not form part of the executive management team, and therefore do not participate in the day-to-day management of the company. However, this detachment from company operations gives them a critical role on the board: they provide fresh objective input on strategic thinking and they monitor the performance of management in the interests of shareholders and stakeholders. Most importantly in this day and age, they provide independent oversight and the underpinnings for good corporate governance, by setting the tone and ensuring the culture of good governance is instituted and sustained across the company.

Nonexecutive independent directors can provide a wealth of domain knowledge, industry experience, and good business judgment based on their varied proficiencies in general management, finance, accountancy, mergers and acquisitions, corporate strategy, law, and so on. Bringing this expertise basket into the boardroom helps increase independent, unbiased, broad-based, and experienced thinking, and can help corporations achieve strategic goals with good governance.

One of the key considerations for nonexecutive independent directors is that they be truly "nonexecutive." A few guidelines help.

In general, a nonexecutive director:

- is not a representative of a shareowner who has the ability to control or significantly influence management;
- has not been employed by the company, or the group of which it currently forms part, in any executive capacity for the preceding three financial years;
- is not a member of the immediate family of an individual who is, or was in any of the past three financial years, employed by the company or group in an executive capacity;
- is not a professional advisor to the company or group, other than in a director's capacity;
- is not a significant supplier to, or customer of, the company or group
- has no significant contractual relationship with the company or group;
- is free from any business or other relationship that could be seen to materially interfere with the individual's capacity to act in an independent manner.

With that background, nonexecutive independent directors are expected to fulfill an important role as custodians of the whole governance process. They are expected to provide input on strategy (constructively challenging and contributing to strategic develop-ment), performance (monitoring the activities of executives, ensuring they meet agreed goals and objectives, and, where necessary, removing senior managers and contributing to succession planning) and govern-ance (providing independent views on resources, appointments, stan-dards of conduct, ethics, CSR, disclosures, and transparency).

The status of nonexecutive independent directors has been ascending given global concerns about corporate governance. After the 2002 US Sarbanes-Oxley Act, for example, the NASDAQ Stock Market introduced a comprehensive package of corporate governance reforms, a response that had far-reaching implications. This covered:

- stock options, with approval by independent compensation committees;
- board independence, with a majority of nonexecutive independent directors, regular meetings, and clarity on payments;

- committees to strengthen nonexecutive independent director roles (such as approving nominations and compensation): audit and compensation committees should consist entirely of independent directors;
- nonindependent directors, whose approval powers and committee involvement were curtailed.

Europe has also been considering the role of nonexecutive independent directors. On May 21, 2003, the European Commission announced measures to modernize company law and improve corporate governance in the EU.[30] Included were objectives for nonexecutive directors:

> In key areas where executive directors clearly have *conflicts of interest* (that is, remuneration of directors, and supervision of the audit of the company's accounts), decisions in listed companies should be made exclusively by *non-executive or supervisory directors* who are in the majority independent. With respect to the nomination of directors for appointment by the body competent under national company law, the responsibility for identifying candidates to fill board vacancies should in principle be entrusted to a group composed mainly of executive directors, since executive directors can usefully bring their deep knowledge of the challenges facing the company and of the skills and experience of the human resources grown up within the company. Non-executive directors should, nonetheless, also be included and specific safeguards should be put in place to deal with conflicts of interest when they arise, for example when a decision has to be made on the re-appointment of a director. [emphasis in original]

Asia, too, has shown increased interest in nonexecutive independent director representation as corporate governance has increasingly taken center stage for the region's companies. Many firms have become ever more integrated with international business, and often reach positions of world leadership in their respective fields. They also face local lawmaking and regulatory pressures to change and, through global exposure itself, encounter foreign investors and new independent stakeholders with demands for performance and good business practices.

Effectively dealing with this onslaught and adapting to new market needs proved difficult for many national champions—Samsung,

Nippon Broadcasting System, Hyundai, and CNOOC quickly come to mind.[31] The original makeup of such successful companies was often based on uniquely local structures such as the *keiretsu* model in Japan, making use of multiple partner cross-company stakeholdings; the *chaebol* model in Korea, with dominant families leading company groups; the state-owned or invested enterprises in China; and the family-owned business model prevalent across much of Asia. Corporate governance within those systems typically catered to local practices and business norms. Acceptance of so-called global governance standards faced stiff resistance until first the 1997–98 financial crisis ushered in required financial discipline and business practice changes, and then the global movement during the 2000s augmented governance standards.

Today the significance of corporate governance is not lost on the region's governments, which have enacted a regulatory support base. The drastic change in the makeup of corporate boards, primarily led by the institution of nonexecutive directors, is indeed striking. Key countries have rushed to increase nonexecutive independent director representation (Japan, Korea, Singapore, Thailand, Taiwan, Hong Kong), a move further pronounced by the substantial number of foreign people on company boards. This has at times had an unsettling effect. Non-national nonexecutive directors typically set out to perform duties as per global corporate board norms, bringing them into conflict with the strategic goals of powerful executive managers. This has led to nonexecutive independent director resignations and change-outs, but also to unpleasant scrutiny for such companies, which as a result have been forced to put the situation right. All this activity has caused a noted shift among corporate powerhouses in the region to restructure and achieve acceptable corporate governance standards.

Unfortunately, along this road to corporate betterment there is a resistance to change lingering under the guise of so-called governance activities. While this process continues, the transparent use of effective nonexecutive independent directors is today being driven more and more by the rules of local financial markets and more importantly by investors, as individuals, funds, and institutions all seek secure and reliable investment growth opportunities.

The biggest challenge to nonexecutive independent directors in Asia remains the overdominant CEO.[32] It is therefore essential that company boards place nonexecutive independent directors in a position where they can truly challenge executive management and focus attention on doubtful practices, even in successful companies. Allowing such independence and position is crucial because nonexecutive independent directors must be able to express views to the board that can be contrary to the CEO's, and critically must be fully confident that as a result they will not suffer any negative consequences.

Another challenge is to reconcile and balance their strategic role with that of monitoring and ensuring good governance. Nonexecutive independent directors should actively give input and help develop a clear strategy by sharing their unique experience and expert knowledge, which may often be new to the executive directors, and giving dispassionate advice. They cannot change or verify every executive directorate and management decision, but they are vital to giving inputs to the strategy and ensuring its implementation.

As regards the control, monitoring, and overall governance function of nonexecutive independent directors, in this changing world where companies are more exposed than ever to public scrutiny, this role has become essential. The ability of nonexecutive independent directors to determine when something is not correct or proper within the company will set them apart and establish their reputation and worth. Asking the tough questions and ensuring that they understand the answers are key. Since nonexecutive independent directors may often have limited knowledge about the company's operations, this must be compensated for through sessions with management and all connected stakeholders to try to get a true understanding of the company's operations and the risks it faces. Ready access to management at separate meetings without the presence of executive management is essential, but all within an agreed framework of work practices with the board. Following are examples of the governance and control functions of nonexecutive independent directors[33]:

- to monitor results, financial and nonfinancial, and demand appropriate corrective action when necessary;
- to ensure that procedures are in place to act as checks and balances for the information received and that all the necessary information has been reviewed to make an informed decision;
- to ask: "is the decision a rational one and in the best long-term interest of the company, rather than the shareholders, employees, or even the directors' pockets?";

- to ensure the maintenance of high levels of compliance and good corporate governance practices;
- to watch over and appraise the quality and effectiveness of executive leadership;
- to ensure that succession planning, particularly for the position of CEO, is in place;
- to serve on and actively contribute to board subcommittees, the most prominent being the audit, remuneration, and nomination committees, it is preferable for an nonexecutive independent director to chair all committees that do not have an executive function.

Another important function of nonexecutive directors is to act as a bridge between management and stakeholders, particularly shareholders. They are expected to defend the company and its executives, but also to listen to the concerns of the stakeholders. It is therefore suggested that nonexecutive directors meet with leading shareholders once a year. Furthermore, they can be viewed as the guardians of the company's reputation by ensuring the company takes a strong ethical position in the market and in the way it conducts its business.

Performing the duties of a nonexecutive independent director is not a box-ticking exercise. It is about being truly independent of management and following the underlying principles of good governance.

Succession planning

The previous sections have discussed the more or less immediate goals for corporations, entrepreneurs, and family business owners, but the crucial issue of succession remains the most daunting challenge for business entities if they are to transcend the next generations.

Succession does not happen overnight—a patriarch doesn't usually hand over his crown to the heir during the last moments of his life. Very often, first-generation owners devote a lifetime of effort and savings and personal sacrifices to make the business successful over the years. The business is a manifestation of their very being and an inseparable part of their lives. As James Thompson, chairman of Crown Group, said in a 2008 discussion with the authors:

The business is much more fulfilling than the money. In my lifetime, I won't sell the business. To see your company destroyed before your lifetime ... I'd rather die first.

He built the Hong Kong-based Crown from scratch in the 1960s, and grew it into a major force in the global relocation industry by the turn of the century. At 68 years old, Thompson is still actively involved in the business and has no strong desire to retire, yet he realizes that there will be the inevitable day when he is no longer able to run the business. He is helping his two children to understand more about the business and wishes they could jointly lead Crown in future. Indeed, provision has been made to the effect that the group business will be split equally between son and daughter after he passes away.[34]

Thompson is among those who think ahead and start planning in advance. Other first-generation owners may not want to let go, and some may still be searching for the ideal successor. Even their family members may find it too sensitive to raise the taboo subject lest they fall out of favor with the patriarch. All these add to the difficulty of a smooth succession. In many cases, a trusted adviser to the patriarch or sometimes an independent nonexecutive director is the ideal person to raise the forbidden subject, and act as the uninterested party who can offer unbiased advice at the critical moment.

Smooth succession requires good planning and the implementation of a multistage process in which the patriarch passes the management and ownership of the business to the successor. Transfer of management begins as soon as the patriarch identifies the candidate and mentors him or her to do the top job. The patriarch may spend years grooming his heir by socializing him or her into the family's business networks.[35] Internationalization is also becoming a preferred strategy for investing in the future successor because any potential problems can be "hushed up" before the reputation and trust of the heir are damaged.

As for ownership, it may be shared equally among siblings or concentrated in the hands of the chosen successor. In the Confucian societies of Asia, the elder son has, with few exceptions, traditionally been the chosen one, although modern-day patriarchs increasingly opt to divide their wealth equally among their children. While this seems fair and can create a solid foundation for harmony, it can also be a hidden trap for discord. When the family grows to the third and fourth generation, the division of wealth leads to fractional ownership and makes the family business more vulnerable to disintegration. Disagreements over business strategies can easily lead to multigenerational feuds that threaten the survival of even those bigger and well-run family businesses. At the other extreme, some of the cousins may not be interested at all in the family business and want to exit by selling their shares secretly to the highest bidders, who may happen to be outside parties.

The family of Eu Yan Sang,[36] a household name for Chinese medicine and herbs in Singapore and Hong Kong, experienced a loss of majority control and court battles involving two family businesses during two decades of feuding. The name of the family business was salvaged only when the fourth-generation cousins agreed not to have any older-generation family members involved as shareholders or board members, and secretly mounted a buyout of the "rival" family business. Reorganizing the family business for a new future, the fourth-generation cousins acknowledged the importance of separating ownership and management. Richard Yu (the current group CEO) said the next CEO did not have to be a family member and executive capabilities should be the most important selection. Since the fifth-generation children are still young, he believed nonfamily members would most likely lead the family business in the next 10–20 years.

"Wealth does not span three generations" is perhaps the most frequently cited comment about family business and fortune. John Ward, a family enterprise specialist at Kellogg School of Management, said the axiom held true in many cases because of the pressure on family rule. Internal risks include succession discord, nepotism, sibling rivalries, and dilution of ownership among the patriarch's many heirs. Externally, home markets are swinging open, exposure to global financial markets is increasing, and minority shareholders are more loudly demanding better governance and higher transparency for publicly traded companies.[37] Yet family businesses are not doomed to fail. The ultimate test is how to make *successive* successions *successful*.

If the family members are determined to continue the business, building in a conflict resolution mechanism and keeping communication frank and open, there is still a good chance that the business can execute long-term strategies for success. A McKinsey report found that there were indeed some key factors contributing to successful succession: strong boards and uncompromising standards of meritocracy in personnel decisions, risk diversification and business renewal through active management of the business portfolio, and long-term financial policies.[38]

Li & Fung, one of the oldest trading companies in Hong Kong, is a good example of how a family-owned business can professionalize its management, diversify its business portfolio, and evolve into a global company. The company was founded in Guangzhou in 1906, initially trading porcelain and silk before diversifying into bamboo and rattan ware, jade, ivory, handicrafts, and fireworks. The first-generation owner sent his second son to set up shop in Hong Kong in 1937. With the influx of refugees after 1949, Hong Kong became a manufacturing economy exporting labor-intensive consumer products. Li & Fung began to export garments, toys, electronics and plastic flowers on top of its original product lines. The company grew into one of Hong Kong's biggest exporters in dollar terms. In the early 1970s, the third generation of the Fung family, Victor and William, returned from education in the US to work at the family firm. Victor (the current group chairman) and William (the current group managing director) worked with their father to modernize and rebuild Li & Fung into a structured business run by professional management at all levels.[39] In a discussion with the authors in 2008 on leadership and family firms, William recalled,

> My father wanted us to bring change to the company. He said we could study the company like an HBR [*Harvard Business Review*] case and make recommendations. So we studied the case and recommended the company to go public. To my great surprise, the family agreed. In 1973, Li & Fung became a public company and we had an independent board and better governance.

In 1985, Li & Fung diversified into the retail business with operations across Asia. In 1989, as a part of the reorganization of the family's interests, Li & Fung was taken private in one of the first management buyouts in Hong Kong. The baton was also officially passed on to the third generation. The company was restructured into two core businesses: export trading and retail. The export trading business was listed on the SEHK in 1992, and from 1995 to 1999 the company continued to diversify into new businesses and expand geographical coverage through organic growth and strategic acquisition. Over 90 years and three generations, Li & Fung has evolved into a truly multinational company engaged in export trading, retailing, and distribution.

When it came to succession, William said that while the fourth generation was involved in the business, the company was run by professional managers at all levels, and personnel decisions were based on meritocracy. An internal candidate suitable for the position of CEO had been identified. "They [the sons] will have to prove themselves to make it to the top. It will be nice to let them succeed but it is not essential. If they want that job, they will come after our candidate," observed William.

Succession is a common issue to all companies, but for family businesses it has until recently been a decision based more on emotion than reason. Trust and family values have tended to bias moguls from choosing a more capable person to fill their shoes. As family-owned firms modernize and emerge from increasing competition in domestic and overseas markets, owners have begun to realize that professional managers in senior positions can fill knowledge gaps and add a new perspective to management decision making. Family business owners are also more aware that a decoupling of ownership and management is crucial for the long-term success of family businesses. There is an increasing trend globally for family firms to look at succession as a process based on true meritocracy, with the top job open to both professional managers and family members. If family businesses in Asia can deal with succession issues in a professional and rational way as nonfamily firms do, we believe that more family firms will survive the third generation and ultimately grow into a new breed of transnational company in the global economy.

MARJORIE YANG, Chair of Esquel Group

"If you can't run a clean operation, you will never be able to run a tight ship."

One of the wonderful things about running a company is you can do things that are transformational. You can start a project today, and the results won't be seen for 10 years. If you are working in a public company you can never do things like that.

(continued)

(*continued*)

One of the things we undertook was to change our company completely from being a quality maker to a quality service provider, a partner to our customers. We wanted to change the entire corporate culture to be a market-oriented, service company that has a long value chain.

It was a big challenge. We started moving people. I lost the CEO. I was chair. I was very happy being chair. Just to remind you, I don't know how to measure you for a shirt. I staple my skirts, and don't know how to sew. And I definitely don't know how to run a garment factory.

I was trying to bring in totally different ways of doing things, and I lost a lot of people.

My father taught me long ago that if you can't run a clean operation, you will never be able to run a tight ship. A lot of companies pay people very little but give them opportunities to make money on the side. That is terrible because you will never get them to focus on doing the right thing.

If you ever get into the habit of paying bribes to get to the end goal, forget it. You will never be willing to work hard. On top of that if we are going to spend a lot of money on IT, using all that fancy information technology equipment, then that information has got to be of good quality.

So we wanted transparency and we wanted 100 percent honesty. That was not the culture in garments.

The management of garment factories traditionally does not really care about its labor. We have made a conscious point on this. Even when we close factories, we have a retraining program. It's very costly for us to close factories.

What do we get in return? Very loyal management. I have one manager who said she was very glad to work for Esquel because she knew I was able to make promises that I could keep. That gets you a lot of payback when your managers feel proud to represent the company.

I think going forward we are going to be making a lot of money because we have done a lot of things that are right. This will allow us, as the total environment becomes one that is more respectful of integrity, to do better and better.

WILLIAM FUNG, Group Managing Director, Li & Fung Ltd.

*"Companies should have a core competency
and should stick to their knitting."*

In 1972, after I finished at Harvard Business School, my brother Victor and I spoke to our mother, who said, if one of you doesn't come home and work with your father ... so I was volunteered by Victor to come back home.

The first thing I said to my dad was, I don't like family companies. I'd been taught all about family companies and nepotism. To my father's great credit he said, you have done this Harvard MBA program, why don't you tell the family what we should be doing to transform ourselves?

Victor was teaching at that time; he was a professor. We studied the company like it was a Harvard Business School case, or a Kellogg case. I told my dad the only way to save the company was to take it public.

I was 22 years old; one of those kids who went straight from college into an MBA. If I had it over again, I would have worked before doing any kind of MBA class. I knew nothing about business, but I thought I did, just like any other business school graduates. The idea was that we can come out and become managing directors.

To our great surprise, the family agreed to go public. It really separated the management and the ownership. We had corporate governance, brought in an independent board, had a regular dividend policy. We took away all the things that brought out the negative side of family businesses.

Also a lot of the positive side. The family transition is interesting. Most businesses start off owned by individuals; in the case of overseas Chinese in particular, they're family companies. And maybe in China now, going forward, there are a lot of family-oriented companies.

In the transition of ownership from the second generation to the third generation, we privatized the company again, in 1989. The second generation had 75 percent of the business, it was a public company. But that transition meant we had to make a general offer anyway.

(continued)

(*continued*)

Victor and I decided to reorganize the company. There's a very influential book, *In Search of Excellence,* where the idea is that companies should have a core competency and should stick to their knitting. Investors like things well defined and clear—the era of conglomerates is pretty much past.

So we decided to separate out all the retail. By that time we were a bit of a small conglomerate. The money we earned on the trading side, we were putting in the retail business, property, ships on charter. We sorted all that out, and kept it a private family company.

Then in 1992, we took the company public again. From then until 2007, almost 20 years, we grew at an annual compounded growth rate of 20 percent. A lot of that had to do with riding a terrific trend of globalization.

JAMES THOMPSON, Chairman, Crown Worldwide Holdings Ltd.

"What I get my buzz out of is watching the company grow."

The three of us make up the executive board. One of the recommendations that was made as a result of the case study by HKUST Business School in August 2007 was to put my kids on the board. Well, they are now coming on the board. It was the right thing to do.

The three of us together make the major decisions and we keep all other managers in the loop very actively.

How do we finance growth? I reinvest the profits. What I get my buzz out of is watching the company grow. I have a comfortable life, but I don't need an airplane to make me happy.

And going public? I have had a lot of free lunches with investment bankers telling me why I should, and had a lot of joy in convincing them they were wrong and I was right. Raising capital through a public offering is certainly a legitimate way. I don't want to do it because things like the regulatory requirements are very onerous and very expensive, and I don't want to go through that.

(*continued*)

I don't think I have to. The company can grow at a nice pace without that. If a big opportunity came along and we didn't have the money to do it, I would just have to swallow hard and say, lost opportunity. Rapid growth isn't always the right way to go.

This goes against the trend in many ways to stay private, but I still feel the most comfortable with this and that's the way I will continue.

Lots of people, when they start up, look for other people's money. Before they know it, they only own 30 percent of the business and one day someone says, I don't like the way you do this so you are out as an operator of this business. I like the control aspect.

We think we know the business better than anyone else and we have our own high level of corporate governance. We wonder what an outsider could contribute. But we are maturing into the fact that probably someone taking a look at us from the outside might say you could do this better or you could do that better. Those things would be healthy for us.

Why haven't we done it yet? We haven't felt the need, but I feel it is a good step in the whole corporate governance process. Maybe if they have knowledge in the financial aspects, the tax aspects, they could keep us from walking into a bad situation.

ANSON CHAN, former Chief Secretary for Administration, Hong Kong Government

"Corporate wisdom is all about accountability, transparency, fairness, integrity, trust, and honesty."

I am sure you all have your own definition of what is meant by corporate governance. It's a concept, a system of control and accountability, and more importantly self-regulation.

Corporate governance as an issue has come to the fore in the past two decades, partly because of competitive pressures, partly because of more concerned consumer demand and higher community expectations.

(continued)

(*continued*)

Frequently, when there are high-profile corporate scandals, such as Enron, the media and the public become very, very exercised about the lack of corporate governance. Then sometimes there is a tendency to be overzealous in terms of government intentions and regulations.

My view is that every corporation requires a system of governance, a system of control, which requires it to be accountable for its actions or its lack of action. But no amount of regulation or control is going to achieve good governance unless there is a culture and a belief—starting with the chairman and the CEO, to the board of directors down to the most junior clerk—that the board of directors, chairman, and CEO are there to act as trustees on behalf of the shareholders, that the shareholders are the true, genuine officers of the corporate, and that the management is there to perform its role as trustee.

Unless there is an acceptance of that, no amount of regulation is going to prevent fraud and human greed.

Greed is not just at the board level. It is sometimes unbelievable how gullible consumers or investors can be because they are attracted by the big dollar signs or they think they are at the end of the rainbow.

The first point I would make about good corporate governance is there has to be a culture of honesty, integrity, a sense of trust, and a sense of moral duty. That trust must be between the management and its employees, also every other stakeholder.

Sometimes there is a tendency to just look at the welfare of shareholders, forgetting that every corporation has other stakeholders like your consumers, perhaps suppliers of goods. Certainly, I think the employee's interest is very important.

Corporations differ in size: there are publicly listed companies; there are private companies; there are SMEs. Clearly, one size, one system of corporate governance will not fit all. You have to have a certain degree of flexibility; you have to adapt the system and concepts to the size and nature of the business. For example, is it a family-owned business? Are there many shareholders? Is the control of the business in the hands of one or two individuals, or are there many, many shareholders?

The most important thing to achieve with good corporate governance is the guiding motive, which I would put this way:

(*continued*)

every corporation ultimately wants to maximize profits, or in other words to create wealth. But the caveat I would put to that is the wealth must be generated and profits must be maximized in ways that are ethical, that are fair to all stakeholders, because I believe in the final analysis that only in this way can any corporation achieve sustainable wealth creation.

Apart from this overarching, cultural motive, there are some basic principles that every corporation must take into account when it decides what it needs to achieve good corporate governance. First, every corporation has to comply with the law. Second, you have the interests of all in mind, not just shareholders, but customers, suppliers of goods, and the community.

Third, all corporations should clearly identify and manage risks. This is particularly important in this fast-changing competitive environment that we find ourselves in today.

Finally, all corporations need to adopt and put in place systems that will help improve quality and efficiency. Decision making must again have regard to the overarching motive, which is that maximizing profits most be done in a fair and equitable manner.

At the end of the day, corporate wisdom is all about accountability, transparency, fairness, integrity, trust, and honesty.

I will leave you with this thought, and that is that over-regulation clearly increases the cost of compliance and can drive away business and investors. There is a growing body of opinion on the Sarbanes-Oxley Act in the US that it has actually driven away businesses, and has helped London become one of the pre-eminent financial centers today, sometimes even overtaking New York.

So it definitely increases the cost of compliance and drives away investors. It creates a minefield for directors if you over-regulate, and creates a goldmine for corporate lawyers and auditors.

Notes

1 Bill Witherell, "The Roles of Market Discipline and Transparency in Corporate Governance Policy," Banque de France International Monetary seminar, May 16, 2003.
2 Ibid.

3 Alan Greenspan, "Corporate Governance," remarks made at the 2003 conference on Bank Structure and Competition, Chicago, Illinois, May 8, 2003.

4 PricewaterhouseCoopers with the Economist Intelligence Unit, "Governance: From Compliance to Strategic Advantage," 2004.

5 Greenspan, op. cit.

6 Harvey Pitt, speech at the Virginia Law School, reported by M. Marshall, www .law.virginia.edu/html/news/2005_spr/pitt.htm, March 28, 2005.

7 Ibid.

8 PricewaterhouseCoopers with the Economist Intelligence Unit, op. cit.

9 Witherell, op. cit.

10 PricewaterhouseCoopers with the Economist Intelligence Unit, op. cit.

11 Donald P. Jacobs, Notes on "Corporate Governance—Boards of Directors," 14, n.d.

12 Deloitte Touche Tohmatsu CPA Ltd., "In the Dark II—What Many Boards and Executives Still Don't Know About the Health of Their Businesses," April 19, 2007 issue.

13 Ibid.

14 Ibid.

15 Ibid.

16 Excerpt from TSMC website www.tsmc.com/english/e_investor/e03_govern ance/e03_governance.htm.

17 Excerpt from TSMC website under Investor Relations/Corporate Governance and Board of Directors.

18 Excerpt from TSMC website under Investor Relations/Corporate Governance

19 Global Views Monthly, "9 Conditions to Build World-Class Corporations," January 28, 2008.

20 Ibid.

21 Roger King, KH-10 class handouts on "Family Business and Entrepreneurship," n.d.

22 Sun Hung Kai Properties, "Corporate Governance—Board of Directors," http:// www.shkp.com/en/scripts/corpgovern/corpgovern_bod.php.

23 TVB News, February 29, 2008

24 James Thompson, KH-10 handouts on "Learning from Leaders," n.d.

25 King, op. cit.

26 ibid.

27 Information from Guest Presentation for KH-10.

28 In 1929, the Dow Jones Industrial Average (DJIA) began its plummet from a high of 386 in September of 1929 to a low of 40.56 in July 1932, an 89 percent drop. Both the market boom and the spectacular crash that ended it have been blamed on the lack of coherent government regulation.

29 Circuit breakers temporarily restrict trading in stocks, stock options, and stock index futures when prices fall too far, too fast. Currently, trading on the NYSE is halted when the Dow Jones Industrial Average (DJIA) drops 10 percent any time before 2.30 p.m., sooner if the drop is 20 percent. But trading could resume, depending on the time of day the loss occurs. However, if the DJIA drops 30

percent at any point in the day, trading ends for the day. The actual number of points the DJIA would need to drop to hit the trigger is set four times a year, at the end of each quarter, based on the average value of the DJIA in the previous month.

30 European Commission, Recommendations on Role of Nonexecutive Directors, 2004.

31 Jean DeSombre, Hong Kong University of Science and Technology Kellogg-HKUST EMBA KH11 Class Presentation, "Agility Logistics Ltd.," April 2007.

32 Ernst & Young Governance & Sustainability Report, 2005.

33 Ibid.

34 Vincent Mak, "Crown Worldwide Holdings Ltd.: Passing the Torch in a Family Business," HKUST, August 2007, 4.

35 Henry Yeung, "Limits to the Growth of Family-Owned Business? The Case of Chinese Transnational Corporations from Hong Kong," *Family Business Review*, vol. XIII, no.1, March 2000, 62.

36 Randel S. Carlock, "Eu Yan Sang: Healing a Family and Business," INSEAD 2006.

37 George Wehrfritz, "Filling the Mogul's Shoes," *Newsweek International*, July 23, 2007.

38 Heinz-Peter Elstrodt, "Keeping the Family in Business," *The McKinsey Quarterly*, no. 4, 2003.

39 Excerpts from company information on www.lifunggroup.com/heritage.

Chapter 7

Building Brands
Across Asia

Why is it that Asia, a fast-growing, brand-crazy region, has produced so few homegrown globally recognized brands? And how can Asian companies build their brands to the level of global superstars and create profitable growth? These are questions that many in the region would do well to ponder. Branding can bolster profitability, but it has been largely untapped by Asian firms.

Although Asia has become the powerhouse driving the world economy thanks to the ascendancy of China and India, when it comes to branding, the story is very different. Look closely at the top 100 Global Brands from *BusinessWeek* and *Interbrand* and you will see many European and North American brands, and notably few Asian ones. Those Asian companies represented are almost entirely from Japan (such as Toyota, Honda, Sony), with a few fast-growing Korean firms (Samsung, Hyundai, LG) rounding out the list (see table 7.1).

Given the size and volume of Asian business today, it is evident that Asia could build many more prominent brands and capture more financial value through better price premiums and customer loyalty. The key to doing that is collaboration. Companies need to expand

Table 7.1: Asian brands in best global brands ranking 2006

Rank	Brand	Country of origin	Sector	Brand value 2006 (mil. $)
7	Toyota	Japan	Automotive	27,941
19	Honda	Japan	Automotive	17,049
20	Samsung	Korea	Consumer electronics	16,169
26	Sony	Japan	Consumer electronics	11,695
35	Canon	Japan	Computer hardware	9,968
51	Nintendo	Japan	Consumer electronics	6,559
75	Hyundai	Korea	Automotive	4,078
77	Panasonic	Japan	Consumer electronics	3,977
90	Nissan	Japan	Automotive	3,108
92	Lexus	Japan	Automotive	3,070
94	LG	Korea	Consumer electronics	3,010

Source: Interbrand.

their focus from chiefly operations, technology, and manufacturing, to one that includes understanding and collaborating with consumers.

Asian "branding" in context

Asia has become the world's biggest manufacturing region and largest provider of commodity products and services. But most of that work is done for other companies. In China, manufacturers produce volume products, and don't have their own strong brand identities. In India, companies provide large back offices to support BPO and text- and voice-based call centers that serve North American or European customers. Most of these products and services are not branded in Asia, and as a result, Asian companies lose out. Instead, the clients of Asian manufacturers and service providers, which are next in the value chain, capture the largest financial share through strong brand strategies and successfully planned and executed marketing programs.

Why, then, do most Asian companies fail to grow global brands? There are several complicating factors:

- Asia is not a homogeneous market like North America. Its uniqueness is in its widespread cultural diversity and preferences and uneven consumption power.
- The nature of Asian business has not always been conducive to branding. Japanese, Korean, and Indian companies are largely conglomerates that span many industries, with limited overlap and synergies. This has been a major impediment to these companies building product brands.
- The mindset in Asia is more geared toward trading, rather than branding, and the focus is on generating revenues, rather than profits.
- Asia has many small, often family-owned businesses, which tend to favor short-term business wins against brand strategies that require more resources and long-term perspectives.
- The lack of intellectual property protection in Asia has been a major barrier to building brands.
- Apart from Japan, Asian economies have not really flourished enough to support a large middle class that is able to buy brands.

A shift on the horizon

Successful brands can be developed, but this requires the understanding and commitment of the whole board, led by the chairman and the CEO, to treat branding as a strategic discipline. This is already starting to happen in some Asian companies.

Competition, globalization, and economic factors are rapidly changing the face of business in Asia. Asian companies that used to manufacture consumer goods cheaply for Western companies are beginning to realize the benefits of branding. In a market where competition implies slashing prices on unbranded products, firms are seeing that competing with other suppliers on cost without any differentiation or loyalty will only lead to a vicious cycle of ever decreasing margins. More and more Asian companies have seen the writing on the wall, and have taken steps to create strong brands that make them stand out from competitors. They have become more attentive to the power of branding in capturing consumers and returning larger profits on their investments.

At the same time, the Asian market is presenting more opportunities. The rising consumption of capital and consumer goods in the region has made Asia the fastest-growing market in the world. American and European branded companies are doing significant business here, particularly in China and India.

Branding to sell across diversity

Asia is a region of many different countries, and each country contains many cultures. Cultural differences can have a major impact on the success or failure of a brand. When companies introduce brands to different cultures, they must find their place on the standardization/ relevance continuum. At one end is the need to maintain a brand image and identity that is consistent with the global brand—this is the very reason for their acceptance across markets. At the other end is complete local relevance, in which a company adopts brand elements, such as images and advertising, that appeal specifically to the tastes and preference of local consumers. A successful global brand treads carefully between these two poles and adopts aspects of each in defining its brand mix for each Asian market.

Companies that have managed to work this continuum and successfully market their brands in Asia include such global names as De Beers, Coca-Cola, PepsiCo, McDonald's, and Disney, and Asian players such as Lenovo, Li & Fung, Sony, Samsung, Hyundai, and Honda. Successful firms typically handle cultural issues very well, such as the tendency in some countries toward certain consumption patterns, and they promote their brands to suit a culturally diverse consumer base.

Companies hoping to cross cultural boundaries with their global brands should bear in mind the following approaches:

Face the challenge of standardization: One of the underlying attractions of branding is that it can reduce customers' search cost and perceived risk by standardizing images, messages, communications, attributes, and features. Consequently, brands generally strive to maintain some consistency in their identity across markets. This standardization forms a fundamental building block for a brand itself, but poses a challenge in cross-cultural situations: how do you adapt a brand to different cultures without diluting the standardization principle?

Take the example of De Beers. A case study on the company that looked at consumer behavior noted the following dilemma:

> A key issue for De Beers was that "Asia" was not a homogenous region, and there was no such person as an "Asian consumer". The more De Beers learned about the different markets through its survey and market research activities, the more it became apparent that pan regional campaigns would not work. Purchasing motivations were driven by different historical and cultural influences. There were sufficient similarities across cultures on which to build regional brand strategies, but equally there were many local nuances to take into account for individual country advertising. Chinese language commercials, for example, had to be in several forms, to cater to Mandarin, Shanghainese or Cantonese speakers, and to readers of complex or simplified Chinese characters.

Innovate to make a brand relevant: Branding in a cross-cultural context is not an insurmountable challenge, though. Firms seeking to build global brands have managed to strike a balance by using innovative means to position their brands in local markets. Instead of following a cookie-cutter approach to branding in each new market, they have evaluated and defined their place on the standardization continuum and made necessary changes to appeal to local tastes and preferences.

For example, PepsiCo has successfully made Pepsi the number one soft drink brand in China and introduced Frito-Lays by adapting the snack to local cultural needs and making it relevant and familiar to people (see Ron McEachern's description of how they did this in chapter 6).

The Chinese company Lenovo acquired IBM's laptop business and transformed the company by making the products relevant to global consumers and building a global brand in quality and state-of-the-art notebook computers.

Collaborate with consumers: The Internet offers brands a very powerful tool to involve customers and bring brands closer to the local culture, by providing people with a platform to interact and collaborate with the brand. PepsiCo has done just that by creating online discussion groups. Similarly, Li & Fung built a global brand in supply chain management by using technology to collaborate with suppliers, customers and employees globally.

Understand consumption patterns: Individualist and collectivist cultures tend to have different kinds of consumption patterns. In individualist cultures, customers make consumption decisions based on their personal choice at an individual level. In collectivist cultures, customers make consumption decisions at a group level, with their family, extended family, network of friends, and even community. These differences hold the key to developing successful branding strategies when entering new markets.

For example, by understanding consumption patterns, PepsiCo was able to design the packaging of Frito-Lays to make it more appealing to consumers and thus encourage them to eat the snack more frequently.

Branding to drive profitable growth

Branding is not just an external exercise. Companies seeking to develop brand identities need to look inward too, to consider the strategy and support they need to help their brands succeed across many countries and tap into the growing Asian markets. Successful cross-cultural branding, and the associated growth in profits, requires organizations to bring into line their goals, strategy, structure, and attitude, as well as the outlook of the leadership team. That may require a firm to transform at least part of the structure of its business.

PepsiCo, for example, transformed its Asian organization by recruiting senior managers and scientists locally, rather than bringing them from overseas. This was because local hires better understood the market, culture, and consumption patterns. Local staff now run subsidiaries in India, China, and other Asia-Pacific countries. Lenovo overhauled its entire organizational structure and changed the primary language in which it conducts business and its workflow process, to align with the global brand it was building.[1]

Companies need to look at what happens on the ground too. An organization needs to be able to collaborate locally at multiple customer touchpoints to make its products and services relevant. PepsiCo used this approach in its R&D. It had one main center in the US that developed products for worldwide consumption, and decided to change to a more distributed structure involving regional R&D centers in China, India, and Australia. The goal was to capture growth opportunities and understand its customers better.

Branding across cultures has challenges, given cultural and linguistic differences, but it can be worth the effort, particularly in a growing market such as Asia. Companies such as De Beers, Lenovo, PepsiCo, and Li & Fung have built strong brands that have captured untapped markets, expanded their consumer base, and extended their geographical reach. With the dramatic growth in the middle class in Asia since the late 1990s, there are historic opportunities for both Asian and global brands to make their marks and lay foundations for long-term growth and profitability.

RON MCEACHERN, former President, PepsiCo International for Asia

"You've got to make marketing do more than just build image."

PepsiCo is now on a massive retooling of our portfolio to create healthier, more nutritious snacks. To take away salt, fat, and sugar—a very North American view about how to make something healthier.

That's not how Asians look at it. They say, what's wrong with sugar—it's got calories in it. What's wrong with oil—give me more. Give me nutritional addition.

Asia is not immune to health and wellness. Asians are becoming less healthy, and obesity and diabetes are becoming problems in places such as China and India. But if we weren't careful, we would have taken our products into Asia and turned them into a North American health and wellness solution, which is not appropriate.

We are working on baked products, light products, and ultimately working on extending our portfolio into nuts, seeds, fruits, and adding local ingredients—honeysuckle, green beans, wolfberry. Talking about wolfberry Quaker oats or wolfberry on a potato chip is totally out of the frame of a North American company.

(continued)

(*continued*)

All this cannot be done from a global brand position. In the past four years, we opened R&D centers in Sydney, Bangkok, Shanghai, and Delhi. And that has fueled most of our success. The competition is fast out here. You can't have integration with your R&D if it is on the other side of the world.

On communication: I believe that advertising and marketing can play a much bigger role in Asia than it does in North America. In North America, it's more imagery building. Out here it's why would I want to eat your product? Who should eat it? When should I eat it? Where should I eat it? How should I eat it? How much of it should I eat? There's a much more holistic sense of communication.

Plus, as you go down to the lower tier cities, the message tends to be different. And you need to engage people in a lot more ways than TV. Asia, and China in particular, is becoming the most sophisticated media market in the world through the Internet, cell phones, alternative communications. You don't just take the Superbowl ad and run it in Asia.

One aside here is personification. Asians love stars—big stars, TV stars. Putting a star in your advertising, an Aaron Kwok, has power. And you can use it to reinforce usage occasions. You can tell me to eat it at college, at the office, during transit, watching TV, surfing the net, doing karaoke.

Internet cafes in China are incredibly successful now. To make it easier to penetrate, in some of these computer halls a little icon will pop up on the computer screens. You don't need to stop playing World of Warcraft. The icon will say, Lays and Pepsi? And a little lady will come over and deliver it right to your terminal.

Interactive media is massive. The usage of cell phones may be lower than in North America, but in absolute numbers, it's huge. Internet penetration, alternative media, integration of your brand into video games—you need to push out into this area and most companies don't have the capability yet. We were finding that even PepsiCo globally was building on what we were doing in Asia.

On sales promotions: we sponsor campus activities. We do sampling at railway and bus stations, cinemas. You need to do more than say, I'm going to do a price promotion. Do a channel, a package, think about how can you make your mark more effectively.

(*continued*)

This is a level of marketing precision that I think they have lost in the US and Europe, where marketing is much more mass reinforcement marketing, rather than brand building, fundamental marketing.

As I mentioned earlier, we are getting into fruit and vegetable snacks, nuts snacks, not just nuts but value-added nuts, rice crackers. This is where you start pushing out from that tiny little slice called Lays potato chips. But this raises another issue. What do you call it? Do you call it Lays?

There's an interesting thing in China called umbrella branding. You buy a famous brand because you can rely on its quality. China, India, Russia, they are looking for a trademark, a brand they can rely on. A couple of big ones are Ting Ying and Want Want, and there are more coming.

Want Want puts hospitals and roadways under the same branding as their rice crackers and gummies. The Chinese are looking for security, health and quality, and recognition among the clutter.

You've got to make marketing do more than just build image. In Asia it has to work harder for you. Product packaging, price promotion, everything has to focus on the consumer and lead them through why.

I call it the "six Ws" research: who eats the product, where, when, what specifically do they eat and why. Go through all of those—and then, Number 6, why not? That's the barrier. The discipline it takes to understand this can be a bedrock.

Note

1 Chen Shaopeng of Lenovo said that to really build an international brand he was forced to spend his days focused on his customers in China and his evenings attending to his dominant markets in the US and Canada. This broad focus changed the way that he and his team worked and expanded their vision.

Chapter 8

Corporate Social Responsibility: Enlightened Self-Interest

Anson Chan, the former chief secretary of the Hong Kong government, refers to corporate social responsibility (CSR) as "enlightened self-interest." Similarly, the UK government has referred to it as "enlightened shareholder value." Skeptics, on the other hand, see CSR as the pursuit of a commercial benefit that a company might receive by raising its reputation with the public or government. So which one is correct?

The straightforward answer could be both. CSR, defined in the web-based encyclopedia, Wikipedia, as the "increasing efforts by organizations to consider the interests of society by taking responsibility for the impact of their business activities on customers, employees, shareholders, communities and the environment in all aspects of their operations," can be good business. It can endear companies to customers, and may also help a firm avoid the expensive consequences of wasteful practices and socially harmful policies.

There are a considerable number of areas that fall within the broad scope of CSR. We will examine some of the most important, including:

- pollution control;
- welfare;
- NGOs;
- gender parity;
- aging population;
- sustainability.

Pollution control

China's success at developing a vast infrastructure and a huge manufacturing base has come at the price of a damaged environment. Air pollution is a serious problem in many parts of the country. The power generation industry has only recently started to control pollutants such as sulfur oxide and nitrogen oxide, which are major contributors to the acid rain that has ravaged many forests. Water quality has also deteriorated. A case in point is Tai Hu, China's third-largest freshwater lake. Green algae appeared in the lake when untreated chemical waste was dumped into it—the local government had turned a blind eye to the situation for the sake of economic growth.

The pollution impacts are spreading across China's borders. The Japanese environmental agency has indicated that air pollutants have blown across the sea and affected nearby nations. The exponential growth of automobiles in China has also contributed significantly to greenhouse gas emissions, further degrading our atmosphere. As leaders within this sector or associated with it, we believe we should ensure that the businesses we deal with are conscious of these issues and cooperate to minimize pollution.

Senior Chinese government officials have begun to put pollution controls in place through China's Environmental Protection Agency (EPA). They are beginning to set better standards, but the lack of enforcement of these standards continues to exacerbate the problem. Unfortunately, the matrix to measure enforcement does not provide incentives for bureaucrats. Businesses are able either to manipulate data or to negotiate lower financial penalties. These practices do not project the seriousness of the EPA and central government's intentions. The incentive to local governments to grow the economy, as part of their performance matrix, also provides a stumbling block in enforcing pollution control.

Ignoring pollution, however, can incur steep financial costs. For decades, rapid economic growth was the priority for governments across Asia, and the developing economies in East Asia in particular have averaged almost 8 percent growth since the 1960s.[1] But while this has brought hundreds of millions of people out of poverty, it has come mostly without regard to environmental protection and sustainability.

The consequences of this are now becoming clear. In China, the world's fastest-growing major economy, environmental degradation was estimated to cost a staggering $64 billion in 2004, or 3.05 percent of its GDP. Even more disturbing is the estimate that 750,000 people die prematurely there each year.[2] Elsewhere, in the ASEAN countries, 6 percent of the forest cover disappeared from 1990–2005, and in Indonesia the figure was 15.5 percent.[3] This is a mind-boggling statistic given the extent of land involved.

What is the relevance of these statistics to business leaders in the Asia-Pacific? Environmental degradation is no longer just a challenge for NGOs or governments—it is also a business challenge. A poor environment can reduce the availability of raw materials, lower worker productivity, and shrink markets. Companies should now develop environment-focused CSR programs to counter this. These programs should not be just public relations projects, but activities that are profitably integrated into their operations. As Anson Chan rightly said, "CSR is enlightened self-interest."

Examples of this "enlightened self-interest" are found at the Dole Food Company, which employs one of the writers of this section. Dole in Asia has an integrated environmental strategy focusing on key areas such as greenhouse gas emissions, energy conservation, pesticide use, and biodiversity. This has forced the company to examine how to protect and conserve the environment while still being a sustainable enterprise.

Dole initiated a returnable plastic crates program called "Crates for Trees" for its Japanese retailer customers. Bananas and pineapples are traditionally exported from the Philippines in cardboard cartons that get thrown away after delivery. Dole started using returnable plastic crates that, after a certain number of return cycles from the Philippines to Japan, are more cost-effective than producing the inexpensive cardboard cartons. Some of the savings are used to fund reforestation projects near Dole's production areas. It is a win–win situation, which also helps retailers to reduce expenses related to garbage disposal.

Initiatives such as this are not just good for saving resources. They also have a part to play in the strategic plans of companies. Anson Chan has also highlighted that "consumer preference for ethical behavior will be a driver in the 21st century." It is now a strategic advantage to have certifications for social and environmental responsibility. Key retailers are starting to insist on environmental and worker-welfare audits before buying anything from their suppliers. Dole has taken pioneering steps toward these certifications in Asia, and in turn has made inroads into the European market.

Pollution control is not just the responsibility of corporations though. Consumers and citizens must also understand the importance and the consequences of a cleaner environment. Pollution control technology is not free—it becomes part of the manufacturing cost—so if consumers only focus on price, manufacturers have no incentive to implement environmental control measures. Consumers should demand "green" products and support a market for these, and corporations should have incentives to use "green" suppliers. The government can support this by providing data, regulation, and enforcement, so that businesses know where they stand.

Pollution control can only be achieved if society as a whole values the results and is willing to contribute to a sustainable environment for their children and grandchildren. As David Bower has said:

> We do not inherit the earth from our fathers. We borrow it from our children.

Welfare

> *Welfare: health, happiness, and fortunes of a person or group, or alternatively, the action or procedure designed to promote the basic physical and material well-being of people in need.*
> —Oxford English Dictionary *online*

A comprehensive welfare system is important both for economic and social reasons. It minimizes the disparity among different social classes, and eases threats of social instability. It also maintains economic momentum in a society where there is an increasing aging population in need of financial and medical care, and fuels productivity among the young through the provision of skills and knowledge.

Just as Asia has enjoyed a honeymoon period of strong economic growth across the region in recent decades, most of its governments are aware of the need to widen social well-being by providing pensions, unemployment aid, medical care, and education. These things are necessary to sustain growth and reduce the possibility of social instability, but they have been patchily applied across the region.

Asian countries differ significantly in the development of their welfare systems, mainly because of their divergent political structures and their varying states of economic maturity. Developed economies such as Japan, Korea, Singapore, and Hong Kong have already established structured welfare systems that span from pension provision, financial aid for the disadvantaged, and free and subsidized education to general medical care for the general population. Welfare programs in these countries are mainly supported financially by the government and funded through various tax or social security schemes, and partly by private enterprise employers.[4]

For the south and southeast Asian countries, such as India, the Philippines, Thailand, Indonesia, and Vietnam, social programs (except for primary education) are usually inadequate and inequitable. Most of these countries have a social security system covering civil servants or workers in the public and private sectors,[5] but individuals working in informal industries, such as domestic servants or farmers, usually miss the welfare safety net.

China, up to the 1980s, had a social security system that was employment based, in which everyone under the Communist regime with "an iron rice bowl" was covered. However, the fastest-growing country in Asia is moving rapidly from a centrally planned economy to a market-driven one, in which many workers have been laid off because of the closing or restructuring of SOEs, and are no longer protected by government-funded social security.[6] China faces profound challenges in establishing a coherent and overarching social protection system, covering retirement, medical care, unemployment, and poverty alleviation.

Against this background, corporate leaders need to consider how they too can contribute to the improvement of welfare institutions in Asia, thus helping to achieve greater stability in the region.

To begin with, corporations must ensure that they provide good working conditions for their workforce, such as reasonable salaries and working hours, a sustainable pension plan, a safe workplace, and adequate coverage of medical needs. In addition, corporations should also invest in training their workers so they can continuously upgrade their skill sets and remain productive in a competitive environment.

Corporate leaders in Asia should also consider taking an active role in contributing to general welfare programs. Donations to NGOs are an obvious way to do this, but companies can also get involved in the rehabilitation and empowerment of the unemployed and under-privileged, for example, by channeling grant money to community organizations involved in job-creation activities, helping schools through grants and volunteers to improve educational quality, and polling existing businesses, new investors, and business development organizations to determine the jobs of the future.

As the great economist Milton Friedman said: "Anything the private sector can do, the government can do worse."[7] Asian executives are leaders in the fastest-growing region in the world, and they are in the best position to promote the betterment of the societies they operate in. And from an economic perspective, corporations that promote adequate welfare in the long run can help to develop a society that is more harmonious and productive, which in turn leads to greater economic returns and, more importantly, to the well-being of all stakeholders.

NGOs

NGOs are often beneficiaries of CSR and corporate donations. It is therefore worthwhile to understand their role in society. NGOs are any nonprofit, voluntary citizens' group organized on a local, national, or international level. They share the same vision as governments—to serve the community—and they tend to operate independently and have tax advantages.

NGOs often act as advisors or fill a niche. For example, NGOs are invited to participate in Singapore's Conference at ministerial level, and they play a leading role at the UN because they have the human resources, capital, and databases to respond quickly to crises. This makes the UN willing to allow NGOs to participate in more activities.

An indicator of the current role of NGOs in Asia is the Asian NGO Coalition for Agrarian Reform and Rural Development (ANGOC). ANGOC is a regional association of 21 national and regional NGO networks from 11 Asian countries actively engaged in food security, agrarian reform, sustainable agriculture, and rural development activities. Its member-networks can effectively reach some 3,000 NGOs throughout the region.[8]

Needless to say, NGOs can hardly do anything without the funding and other support that enable them to implement development, relief, and rehabilitation activities in developing countries or regions. Governments are often partners and contribute funds to NGO aid programs in target countries. Many governments, however, do not allow foreign countries to fund their own countries' NGOs.

Government funding rarely covers all the costs though, so NGOs also turn to corporations for support. The private sector is an important source of funding and assistance and many companies are willing to support non-profit work to fulfil their CSR obligations.

One example of corporate giving is China Overseas Holdings Ltd., which employs one of the writers of this chapter. In January 2008, when snowstorms blanketed China's Yangtze River region leading to a direct loss of RMB150 billion and more than 100 deaths, China Overseas contributed HK$2 million to Hong Kong Oxfam to provide relief. This brought the company's total charitable sponsorships to more than HK$70 million.

Gender parity

No country has ever achieved gender parity, even though as a global issue it transcends nationality, religion, and race. The latest report by the World Economic Forum,[9] which ranks 128 countries around the world on four gender parity measures—economic participation and opportunity, educational attainment, political empowerment, and health and survival—clearly shows a significant variation between countries. The Nordic nations are consistently on top (led by Sweden), while many Middle Eastern countries, from impoverished Yemen to wealthy Saudi Arabia, are ranked lowest.

Although there are consistent improvements in most of the countries surveyed, plenty of work still needs to be done by most governments, NGOs, business leaders, and society as a whole to close the gap. According to the report, while only 25 countries failed to improve their score, even top-ranked Sweden had a score of only 0.8146 (a score of 1 represents total equality between men and women).

The gender gap can be critiqued on different levels. The most obvious may be the moral view; that is, the belief that all humans are born equal, that men and women should have equal rights and equal opportunities. However, as business leaders in Asia, we would like to highlight here the economic logic for closing the gender gap, especially in the burgeoning Chinese economy.

In the 2007 Global Gender Gap Report, China's overall score was 0.664, ranking it 73rd (out of 128; see figure 8.1). The data reveals interesting information: The Economic Participation and Opportunity sub-index (overall ranking, sixtieth) shows China scored above average for the female to male ratio for labor participation (0.86 against the world average of 0.69), professional and technical staff (0.82 against 0.68), and income and wage equality for similar work (0.69 against 0.64). However, China's government and businesses should pay attention to the low female to male ratio for legislators, senior officials, and managers (0.14 against the world average of 0.26). By contrast the Philippines' ratio is 1.38.

With these figures in mind, consider the results of the survey of 214 executives in Asia by the Kellogg-HKUST Executive MBA program, described in the introduction to this book. The executives were asked to rank the top challenges for China's future growth. They said recruiting talented local managers was a major concern. If this holds true for others, China's government and the business community cannot afford to ignore the large pool of women in their search for talented managers and employees. This is unexploited talent, and it is a crucial resource for a fast-developing country such as China.

The government and the business community in China need to create an environment and opportunities that are "women friendly." Large corporations and SOEs can do more to empower women by providing more opportunities for them and creating paths for them to

Figure 8.1: China's scorecard

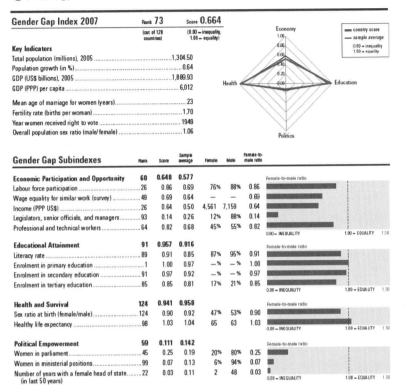

Source: Gender Gap Index 2007 and the IMF's World Economic Outlook Database 2007 available at http://www.IMF.org/weo. The Global Gender Gap Report 2007 is published by the World Economic Forum.

move into roles that were once out of reach. Large corporations can lead by example through their policies on women's salaries, maternity leave, and career development (including for those returning from maternity leave).

The Chinese government, meanwhile, could tackle the low prominence of women in senior positions. In the Political Empowerment sub-index, China ranked 59th overall. In terms of women in parliament, it was 45th, but for women in ministerial positions, a very low 99th of 128 countries.

The government needs to set an example for the business world by promoting and increasing the opportunity of women to lead the country in significant positions. We believe that the appointment of more female officials in high positions should follow China's current trend of nominating younger high-ranking officials. This should be more than a symbolic move. Women should occupy positions of power where they can influence and drive matters important to women.

Education is another area where gender parity should matter to business. China ranked 91st in the Educational Attainment sub-index, with sharp divisions evident between different educational sectors. In primary education, China achieved a perfect score of 1, alongside such countries as Australia, Canada, Japan, and the UK, but it does not do so well for secondary education (91st) and tertiary education (85th). In terms of overall literacy it is ranked 89th, posing a significant threat to the country's fragile social fabric.

However, globally, including in China, the fastest gender gap reductions are happening on the educational front. This should help women gain training in relevant and needed professions and open the door to influential managerial, legislative and technical positions. For that to happen, the business community, government, and NGOs will need to invest significantly in educational initiatives for women and encourage them to enter traditionally "male-only" professions.

A final area worth noting in gender parity is health. On the Health and Survival sub-index, China ranked 124th overall, only four places from the bottom of the list. The female to male gender ratio of 0.9 (meaning only 47 percent of the population is female and 53 percent male) highlights the known issue of male gender preferences. With the One Child Policy and the traditional preference for a male heir, it is believed many female babies are abandoned as orphans or, worse, are victims of infanticide. The responsibility for changing this lies with the government, starting with a rethink of the One Child Policy. Perhaps families whose firstborn is a daughter could have more than one child, or those who want more than one child could do so until a male baby is born. These policies could be supported by stricter law enforcement and monitoring of illegal abortions.

This fight must not be the government's alone. NGOs can increase public awareness, and educate the public about the issues involved. The business community could better integrate women into the business world, thereby improving the economic status of single females as well as families (and specifically those with female children only) and reducing the necessity for male heirs. The economic improvements that would come through having more women in the labor force, with equal rights, would be significant.

Whatever the reasons for gender inequality in China, one thing is certain. If China wishes to keep growing at its breakneck pace, it must actively find ways to improve opportunities for women. This makes good business sense, both for companies and governments. As the data in figures 8.2 and 8.3 indicate, there is a positive correlation between a country's global competitive advantage and GDP, and its ability to close the gender gap. China is already enjoying spectacular growth as the world's manufacturing powerhouse. Can you imagine how much more dominant it would be with a smaller gender gap?

Aging population

Today, in the developed world, the elderly (defined as people aged 65 and over) comprise 15 percent of the total population; by 2030, the figure

Figure 8.2: Global Competitiveness Index vs. Gender Gap Index

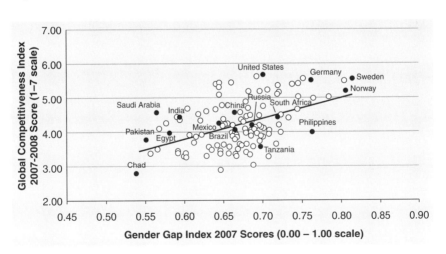

Source: Gender Gap Index 2007 and Global Competitiveness Report 2007–2008.

Figure 8.3: GDP per capita vs. Gender Gap Index

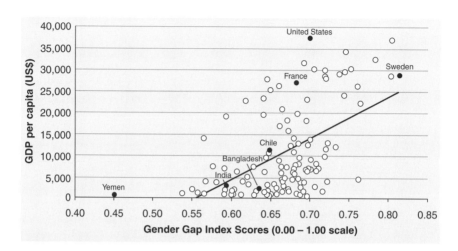

Source: Gender Gap Index 2007 and the IMF's World Economic Outlook Database (April 2007), available at www.imf.org/weo; Luxembourg has been removed.

will be about 25 percent. With an older population come extra costs to provide health care and pensions—a situation compounded by earlier retirement, inadequate personal savings, and declining levels of family support. Many countries are trying to figure out how to pay for these things. Worryingly, the problem is also spreading beyond developed countries to places such as China, which is projected to have developed-world levels of old-age dependency by the middle of the century.

Aging populations are a global challenge for governments and businesses, which need to devise strategies to not only pay the extra costs, but also to tackle the problem of an aging workforce.

The current situation has its roots in falling fertility and increased longevity. Worldwide, the fertility rate has fallen from 5.0 to 2.7 since the mid-1960s. Meanwhile, since World War II, global life expectancy has risen from about 45 to about 65. In developed countries, life expectancy has risen from the mid-to-high 60s to the mid-to-high 70s, and in a few countries, including Japan, it has passed 80. As a result, there are fewer young people and more elderly.

Many Asian countries will face a significant aging of their populations over the next few decades. In 2004, more than 9 percent of Asia-Pacific's population was 60 or older, but by 2050 that figure will reach 23.5 percent. The situation is particularly acute in China, which has 39 percent of the region's population and the lowest population growth rate (due to the one child policy introduced in 1979 to curb China's then booming population). Its 130 million elderly residents now make up a little more than10 percent of the population, but that is predicted to rise to more than 31 percent in 50 years. The implication is that the working population will be stretched to provide for those who have retired. A growing number of single young people are facing the daunting prospect of caring for parents and four grandparents—a phenomenon known as a 4–2–1 family.

Japan has already seen a dramatic demographic shift: its birth rate is 1.29 and falling, while its baby boomers started reaching the retirement age of 60 in 2007. Japan's demographic crisis raises three major issues: 1) how to sustain the pension system, 2) whether to allow more immigration, and 3) the heavy burden on smaller numbers of taxpaying workers to support an increasing number of retired beneficiaries. The shrinking workforce may yet force Japan to accept large-scale immigration.

Korea faces similar problems, and has actively implemented a new pension law and new programs that provide benefits for having children. On the corporate side, organizations are also taking action. They are preparing new retirement plans that encompass the new pension law, changing their human resources management to be based on job value rather than seniority, and turning to more work–life balance benefit programs, which help women stay in the workforce.

Other countries should learn from these examples. The aging population "crisis" will increase government expenditure, and could undermine national savings and economic growth. Governments therefore need to re-examine and adjust their healthcare systems, state pensions, and social security schemes.

Businesses also need to take action. An aging workforce has implications for talent recruitment and management. More generally, it is worth bearing in mind that as the workforce ages, developed countries may experience widespread labor shortages, which in turn will give rise to extraordinary new immigration pressures.

Sustainability

Sustainability, or to use its full term, sustainable development, is gaining increasing strategic importance for governments and organizations. It can be defined as a combination of:

- maintenance of high and stable levels of economic growth and employment;
- social progress that recognizes the needs of everyone;
- effective protection of the environment;
- prudent use of natural resources.

This sounds fantastic news for the environment and for society. However, if the aims of organizations are to generate wealth and to maximize shareholder value, then the obvious challenge is how to integrate environmental considerations into their mainstream businesses and business strategies, that is, how to deal with operational impacts on the environment, such as energy and raw material use, waste, and transport, while maximizing shareholder value.

It's a worthy aim, but not an easy one to achieve. Corporate sustainability requires that companies not only look after their own backyards, but also apply sustainability assessments to their customers and suppliers to ensure they too are managing these issues. Implementation is also an issue. It is one thing to have CSR strategies, another to implement them. How do you measure success and how do you ensure that the corporate culture supports a CSR strategy?

CSR as a subject sent one writer of this chapter scurrying to find out what his company had done on the subject.

My Company's Approach to CSR

Of course, like many of you, I have heard of CSR and I knew what the acronym stood for, but little else. Yet I could not recall seeing or hearing of a policy on CSR at my organization. Had we fallen at the corporate culture hurdle?

After doing some research, I now know such a policy exists. However, our well-drafted and glossy policy is not an implemented strategy[10]—although it does make interesting reading, with a definition and background similar to that used in this chapter. It sets out three key objectives.

'The aim...is to safeguard the organization's assets and reputation, whilst encouraging the development of responsible business.... Objectives are as follows:

1. Stewardship & Responsibility—playing our part in the financial services sector:
   (a) Progressive integration of environmental and social considerations into business decisions.
   (b) Establish relevant performance indicators along with associated improvement targets.
   (c) Publish relevant information about our environmental performance.
   (d) Raise awareness amongst staff, undertake dialogue with stakeholder groups (including investors, regulators and suppliers) and play a part in community initiatives.
2. Compliance, Environmental Risk & Pollution Prevention—operating responsibly:
   (a) Minimize waste and promote efficient use of energy, raw materials, manufactured products and natural resources.
   (b) Maintain management systems that ensure high standards of environmental performance, conserve resources, prevent pollution and meet regulatory environmental standards.
3. Product & Business Development—working with our customers and business partners:
   (a) Encourage the development of products and services from partners and suppliers whose environmental policies are compatible with our own.
   (b) Develop new products and services, which seek to achieve greater sustainability.
   (c) Convert environmental risks into sustainable business opportunities for our customers and the group.'

My company lets stakeholders know how we're doing against our objectives in an annual social responsibility report, which forms part of the annual accounts and includes commentary from the chairman and CEO. For example, we have reduced our CO_2

(*continued*)

(continued)

footprint by more than 200,000 tons, moved to recycled paper globally, arranged financing for renewable energy companies, provided financial training to schoolchildren, and extended loans to 39 percent of small businesses in the UK's 5 percent lowest wards. Perhaps more relevant to the Asia-Pacific region is the information the company has provided on the number of project finance deals transacted in accordance with the Equator Principles.[11]

To conclude, sustainability and the efforts of organizations to balance social and environmental responsibility with the economic responsibility of creating shareholder value can only be positive things. Furthermore, we envisage that as customer awareness grows (and very possibly that of the supply chain) there will be a greater necessity for companies to demonstrate active CSR. Companies that ignore it and do not integrate it into their strategy will lose their competitive edge (including in the eyes of their employees).

ANSON CHAN, former Chief Secretary for Administration, Hong Kong Government

"The strongest motivator is…enlightened self-interest."

Economist and Nobel Laureate Milton Friedman once said there is no such thing as CSR; that corporations exist simply to create wealth and to maximize profits. So long as they do that in ways that are not infected or fraudulent, that is all that one should expect from them.

That may be a purist view. I take a much broader view, and it is this: if you look at social responsibility, every individual has a responsibility to society and to the community in which he or she lives. Today, with globalization, every individual has a social responsibility to the world at large. That responsibility goes for corporations, for organizations—that you have a duty to ensure that the services and the products that you provide are provided in such a way that it does not bring harm to the community as a whole.

(continued)

Therefore, I think, every corporation does have a social responsibility. But that social responsibility, that sense of playing fair by your customers, shareholders, the community is something that has to be done voluntarily. It isn't something that can be dictated or mandated by law or by government.

As with a lot of things, at the end of the day, the strongest motivator for having a sense of social responsibility is what I would call enlightened self-interest. In other words, if a business accepts that it is good business sense to demonstrate that it has CSR, it actually helps in cultivating and maintaining customer satisfaction and customer loyalty. That helps you in brand differentiation and keeping the brand's reputation, and you look at companies that produce goods because the goods are known to be based on a set of ethical values.

For example, the Body Shop has been able to sell its products because it believes in a certain way of manufacturing products that people will buy.

Increasingly, in the twenty-first century, consumer preference for ethical behavior and for companies that have both good governance and corporate social responsibility will drive companies more and more to take over social responsibility.

In Hong Kong, I have the impression that MNCs are frequently told by their headquarters that you must do something about social responsibility. Usually this boils down to maybe a few people in the company saying, yes, we will plant a few more trees, make more donations to charity; we might organize walks, and so on.

Across the board as a whole, CSR as a well accepted concept is certainly not well understood by corporations. Usually, when the government tries to stimulate interest in CSR, it is always a few big companies that turn up who are already practicing this. Very few companies, certainly very few small-to-medium concerns, turn up.

I don't think that CSR as a concept will be introduced very quickly. It is something that will take time for companies to accept, particularly to come to accept as part of very good business.

As managers, however, you have to ask to ask yourself what makes good managers. I think CSR is part of what makes a good business manager. You are there to produce goods and services

(continued)

(*continued*)

in ways that are fair, equitable, and accountable. You are there to manage risks, to manage reputation, to protect and cultivate integrity.

There are pressures all around corporations to adopt CSR because of heightened consumer expectations, but also I think a vigilant and robust press. They will press companies to go down the road of CSR because that is the only way to survive, and in the long run to stay in business and to make a profit.

I hope that as managers, if you embrace this concept, it is something that you can sell to your employees. I don't think it is anything you can sell to your consumers because they will be demanding it if you don't provide it. It goes beyond just doing the odd charity project.

The Hong Kong government at one stage tried to get companies to do more in the sense of corporate social responsibility. At one stage, it set up what was called a partnership fund . . . but businesses simply were not interested. They didn't buy into it.

This just underlines the point that CSR as a concept will only exist when businesses realize it makes good business sense and it is in their own business interests to adopt it.

Notes

1 Lawrence J. Lau and Jungsoo Park, "The Sources of East Asian Economic Growth Revisited," Stanford University and the State University of New York at Buffalo, September 2003. http://www.stanford.edu/~ljlau/RecentWork/RecentWork/030921.pdf.

2 Richard Welford, "China's Environmental Degradation Creating Social Time Bomb," CSR Asia, 2007.

3 Asian Development Bank, Key Indicators 2007, 2007. www.adb.org/statistics.

4 Raymond Chan, "The Sustainability of the Asian Welfare System after the Financial Crisis: Reflections on the Case of Hong Kong," Southeast Asia Research Center–City University of Hong Kong, The Working Paper Series No. 7, 2001.

5 D. Renjini, "Welfare Capitalism in Southeast Asia," *Social Security, Health and Education Policies Journal of Third World Studies*, Spring 2003.

6 Joe C.B. Leung, The emergence of social assistance in China, *International Journal of Social Welfare*, 2006, 15 (3), 188–198 doi:10.1111/j.1468-2397.2006.00434.x

7 Milton Friedman, "The Social Responsibility of Business is to Increase its Profits," *The New York Times Magazine*, September 13, 1970.

8 Asian NGO Coalition website, http://www.angoc.ngo.ph.

9 The Global Gender Gap Report 2007 is published by the World Economic Forum. The Global Gender Gap Index 2007 is the result of collaboration with faculty at Harvard University and University of California, Berkeley.

10 The final note, under the heading "Scope," reads "This policy applies to all staff."

11 The Equator Principles are a set of standards and principles that "act as a benchmark for the financial industry to manage social and environmental issues in project financing." See www.equator-principles.com.

Chapter 9

Learning from Our Leaders

When we first embarked on this book, the clouds of economic turmoil were only just becoming discernible on the horizon. The chief preoccupation of most managers at that time was how to make the most of the opportunities that seemingly abounded—how to get the right people in place, succeed in the right markets (especially China), encourage innovation, all while being a good corporate citizen. That was early 2008. Today, the landscape looks a lot different. Or so it seems.

The financial tsunami that began to hit in September 2008 quickly focused attention on survival. Businesses across the globe have taken an unprecedented battering. Many have seen their profits wiped out, and have had to lay off staff. It may be hard in such an environment to envisage that the chief concerns of leaders should be talent retention or innovation. But these topics are at the heart of survival and long-term sustainability for any business.

That's not only my opinion. My introduction to this book reports on a survey of alumni of the Kellogg-HKUST EMBA program, who all hold or have held senior positions in many different industries across Asia. They were asked to rank eight leadership challenges facing executives in Asia in early 2008. You may recall that talent and retention came tops (31 percent), followed by China strategies (18 percent), globalization (14 percent), economic and political stability (12 percent), innovation (also 12 percent), corporate governance (7 percent), marketing strategies (6 percent), and CSR (less than 1 percent). Well, we repeated the survey in December 2008 and March 2009 with two recent intakes of students and found some fascinating shifts.

The December survey reflected concerns at the time that the global basis of trading and financing was under threat: globalization was most frequently cited as the top challenge (24 percent), followed by innovation (20 percent), marketing (16 percent), stability (15 percent), talent (11 percent), China (5 percent), CSR (3 percent), and corporate governance (0 percent). (Let's just say the survey was conducted immediately before the Bernie Madoff scandal erupted.)

Then in March, when things had calmed down, and companies and governments had started making adjustments, the focus turned firmly to strategies for survival. Innovation was ranked number one (27 percent), reflecting the view that firms can stay competitive by being innovative. Next came talent (18 percent), stability (18 percent), marketing (16 percent), globalization (10 percent), corporate governance (5 percent), and CSR and China (both 1 percent).

If there is anything to read into the variations of these surveys, it's that leadership is very situation specific. Leaders need to understand the places and the situations in which they operate. They need to be on the lookout for trends and seek input so they can stay ahead in their markets. The top business leaders in Asia have been remarkably flexible and responsive in this respect over the years. Their sights are usually set on what they should do next.

And this is where *Learning from Leaders in Asia* has value. This is a book written by Asian-based executives who, even in this topsy-turvy world, know which issues leaders need to consider to help their companies achieve success.

Our authors tell us that innovation, which ranks so highly now, started to become a feature of several Asian powerhouse firms after the 1998 Asian financial crisis. Companies such as Samsung, Lenovo, Taobao, Asus, and Li & Fung expanded from Asia into other markets by differentiating themselves and paying close attention to the markets and cultures they were operating in. Their innovations were adapted to their markets, not the other way around. Closely related to innovation is branding (or marketing), where the same demands of differentiation and cultural sensitivity apply. These are lessons that surely hold up as equally under today's constrained economic conditions as they did in boom times.

Talent retention, that eternal quest, has some special challenges in Asia. Cultural understanding is especially important, say our authors, many of whom work in multicultural environments where companies are developing strategies to cultivate local talent with a global outlook. So, interestingly, is company reputation. The authors cite surveys that show people in Asia want to work for high-quality, reputable, and ethical business organizations. Compensation and career paths matter too, but the intangibles may be even more important. That's something to consider in light of two other chapters, on corporate governance and CSR. The respondents in our surveys should perhaps give these two issues more weight, since they may be factors in whether a firm can attract and retain talent with leadership potential. Something to think about.

Stability has become a bigger concern among executives for obvious reasons. What's interesting is that our authors examine stability in Asia. The issues are somewhat different here than in North America or Europe. Domestic markets are still nascent, and there is still a lot of groundwork to be done in infrastructure. The situation in each country varies and our writers advise business leaders to master the context—know who and what you are dealing with. It's a theme that runs through several chapters. Solutions seen elsewhere may not work in Asia, in fact the challenges may be completely different and require a whole other approach. Even in an economic downturn.

The final two areas that our authors cover are China and globalization. Judging by their ranking in the March 2009 survey, you might think these had become of minor consequence (they were ranked second and third, respectively, in early 2008, and fifth and eighth in 2009). I think that's a risky view to take. The lessons from these chapters is that Asian companies are managing to move beyond being the "world's factory" to establishing themselves as global firms in their own right. Focusing on China and globalization may seem a little out of joint with more immediate concerns, but regard them as sleeping giants. As the global economy rebounds—and it inevitably will—these topics will again move to the forefront, and leaders need to be prepared.

It is that idea of preparation and staying abreast of new developments that underscores successful leadership. Leadership is about the future. Spotting trends and "sense making" are critical, and require leaders to reflect on the past and believe in the value of lifelong learning: learning from others, learning from books, learning from business schools, learning from mistakes—learning in all its forms. Perhaps one thing we can learn from the recent downturn and the excesses of Wall Street is that the world is crying out for responsible leadership, one that has regard for the new triple bottom line: profits, people, and the planet!

Addendum

At the end of this book is a recent case written by Isabella Chong under my supervision, which is used in the HKUST EMBA and MBA programs. I have included it here because it illustrates important issues that all leaders, especially those in Asia, are facing. The case concerns the Link Real Estate Investment Trust, a Hong Kong outfit that transitioned from government owned to privately owned, and the trade-offs it had to make. Many Asian countries, especially China, are undergoing a similar transition and similarly have to make trade-offs, particularly among different stakeholder groups. Concluding our book with this case allows the reader to consider the insights from this book in the context of a real-life Asian leadership situation.

When I use the case for teaching, I split the students into various special interest groups and hold a class debate. We then consider all points of view, much as any leader in any diverse entity must do on a regular basis. The Link case is an ideal example of the complexities involved in managing inputs from different sides, while staying focused on the principles so necessary for responsible leadership.

Appendix 1

Introducing Our Distinguished Speakers

KH10 Graduation

Anson Chan

Former Chief Secretary for Administration,
Hong Kong Government

Anson Chan

Anson Chan has been a prominent political figure in Hong Kong for many years. She was the first Chinese and first woman to become chief secretary for Administration in 1993 and she held that post after 1997, making her the second most senior government official after Chief Executive Tung Chee-Hwa.

She retired in 2001 after almost 40 years in government service, during which she dealt with finance, the economy, commerce, industry, the civil service, and social services.

In 2007, she ran in a by-election for Hong Kong's Legislative Council (LegCo) and won. She stepped down at the next full LegCo election in 2008, but remains active in the political scene, underscoring her commitment to democracy.

There's a belief in Hong Kong that going too far down the road to democracy leads to instability and bad governance, that business should be running the place. I beg to differ. I believe that democracy is very good for business. If you look at some of the failures that have occurred in the past four to five decades in Hong Kong, they were not caused by the government, they were caused by business.

Democracy is not a panacea for all ills. Those who come from fully fledged democracies realize that. Until somebody creates a system that is better, I think it is still the best on offer in terms of stability, accountability, and fulfilling community aspirations.

In China, it is true that the country as a whole is not a democracy and it will be some time before it becomes one. But there has been a degree of liberalization.

To their credit, the leadership at the center has been able to manage the rapid economic transformation that has taken place through a growing awareness that the party has to grow closer to the people. That the leaders have to be seen to be taking into account the people's mood and aspirations, in order, if nothing else, to justify the continuation of the one-party system.

Chan has a Bachelor of Arts (Honors) from the University of Hong Kong. In 1999, she was awarded the Grand Bauhinia Medal by the Hong Kong government, and in 2002, she was appointed an honorary Dame Grand Cross of the Most Distinguished Order of St. Michael and St. George by Queen Elizabeth II.

* * *

Chen Shaopeng
President, Lenovo Emerging Market Group; Senior Vice President, Lenovo Group

Chen Shaopeng is one of China's foremost business leaders. He was a prominent member of the Lenovo team that worked on the acquisition of IBM's Personal Computer Division in 2005, and has played a key role in the growth and development of Lenovo into one of China's flagship companies.

Chen Shaopeng

Chen started his career in Lenovo as a sales representative, and rapidly rose through the ranks. He has had a formative role in helping to lead the organization through constant change and evolution in the rapidly changing Chinese environment, and also helped Lenovo establish itself as one of China's first truly multinational companies.

When I first joined the management team of the Lenovo world-wide group, due to the language barrier, I was very quiet. I went through the beginning of my journey with a little bit of doubt. Do I really want to become a global executive? It was hard.

I realized two things were very important. The first was confidence. I tried to learn more and more, and I grew from being quiet to being actively engaged. It was a process of increasing my confidence.

The second was to proactively contribute to the team. If you do not contribute, you do not gain trust. First I had to trust others then I had to gain their trust. Confidence and contribution were the keys for me in this journey.

What I have learned in the process is that you need three things to succeed. The first is ambition. If you do not have a big ambition, you cannot sustain your progress. The second thing is courage. If you have ambition, change is always difficult and you need the courage to overcome the challenges. The last thing is continuous learning. That means you should be open-minded. If you already have a strong belief in your current success, you may not learn more or grow quickly.

Chen has used that approach to, among other things, develop Lenovo's brand equity. One of the keys in this has been the sponsorship of major sporting events, including the 2008 Beijing Olympic Games.

Chen is a graduate of Beijing Technology and Business University and holds an EMBA from Tsinghua University.

* * *

Steven J. DeKrey

Senior Associate Dean and Director of MBA/EMBA/MSc Programs, HKUST Business School

Steven J. DeKrey

Professor Steven DeKrey has tackled leadership issues from every angle—as a leader himself, as a research academic and as an educator. He is Chairman of the Board of Governors of the American Chamber of Commerce in Hong Kong, and is widely recognized across Asia as an expert in leadership development and personality assessment.

He came to Hong Kong in 1996 from the US, where he completed a PhD in psychology at the University of Iowa before obtaining an MBA from Kellogg

School of Management at Northwestern University. He went on to become Assistant Dean and Assistant Professor at this world-renowned business school. In 1989, he joined the University of Florida as director of MBA programs before joining HKUST as Associate Dean and Director of Masters programs.

Under DeKrey's leadership, the nascent HKUST postgraduate programs have made remarkable advances. The Kellogg-HKUST Executive MBA was established in 1998 with DeKrey as Founding Director and is now ranked number two in the world by the *Financial Times*. The full-time MBA is ranked number 17 globally.

> In a very short time we have made considerable progress in establishing high-quality programs that produce leaders who can serve Asia and the wider world. There is considerable talent and energy out here, and my job is to help people harness that so they can be effective and accomplished leaders. I think our standing in the *Financial Times* is strong evidence that our approach is working.
>
> Now, with *Learning from Leaders in Asia*, we hope these leaders can share their insights with a new generation and pass on the mantle.

DeKrey is frequently invited to speak on leadership topics and emotional intelligence, and to participate on judging panels such as the Asian Wall Street Journal Asian Innovations Award. He is also active in community organizations, such as the Kellogg Alumni Club of Hong Kong, the Rotary Club and Junior Achievement Hong Kong, and was Chief Judge of the 2009 Hewitt Best Employers awards.

* * *

William Kwok Lun Fung

Group Managing Director, Li & Fung Ltd.

William Fung and his brother Victor have been dubbed "the great middlemen of modern trade" by *Time* magazine for their success in organizing the production of goods on a global scale.

Over almost 40 years, they helped their family-owned company Li & Fung go public, then private, then public again as they grew the

William Kwok Lun Fung

firm into a major supply chain manager dealing in a wide range of consumer goods.

The company was started by their grandfather in 1906 for products associated with the old China trade, such as porcelain and silks, and moved into consumer goods under their father's direction. William and Victor were asked to help run the company in the early 1970s and returned to Hong Kong from the US, where they were educated. William earned a Bachelor of Science in Engineering from Princeton and an MBA from Harvard.

As they steered the company into supply chain management, the brothers saw opportunity in globalization. They realized that with modern transportation and information technologies, their operations no longer needed to be based in one country. They pursued what William has called "borderless manufacturing."

> Li & Fung is like an orchestrator for different suppliers and manufacturers. It was once put to me that we had moved up the supply chain. I thought about that for a while. The difference between the old supply chain of my grandfather's time was that all the players in the supply chain were adversaries—they had buying and selling relationships, which meant if I had yarn and I sold you some at a cheap price, you sort of won.

> The supply chain today is a cooperative one. It's a partnership arrangement. It requires a terrific amount of trust and sharing of responsibility down the whole supply chain. The idea is that nobody makes money unless you satisfy the ultimate customer and you beat the other guy's supply chain.

Li & Fung operates more than 80 offices in more than 40 economies in North America, Europe, and Asia, and in 2007 had turnover of more than $11 billion. In 2008, William and Victor also co-authored a book with Yoram (Jerry) Wind on their company, *Competing in a Flat World: Building Enterprises for a Borderless World.*

* * *

Ron McEachern
Former President, PepsiCo International for Asia

Ron McEachern has deep experience in consumer products and selling brands in Asia. He worked with PepsiCo for 23 years before retiring as President of PepsiCo International for Asia in 2008.

Ron McEachern

"My hip pocket strength is with marketing," he says, which he has padded out over the years by developing expertise in innovation, brand development, and corporate social responsibility.

McEachern started out in Canada where he worked with Procter & Gamble for nine years in marketing, and acquired an MBA from York University.

His move to PepsiCo brought him high-flying assignments in North America and Europe, including Senior Vice President for Canada and Central US, President of Pepsi-Cola Beverages Canada, and Region Vice President for Pepsi-Cola International in Western Europe, before his posting to Asia in the mid-1990s.

As President of PepsiCo International for Asia, he oversaw the introduction of many brands new to Asia, and even new ways of eating such as his innovation with Lays potato chips (see chapter 6). At the end of his tenure, PepsiCo Asia spanned more than 80 separate company-owned, franchised, and publicly listed entities and 40 separate joint ventures in mainland China generating annual sales revenues of more than US$4 billion.

> The consumer market in Asia is more complex and sophisticated today. It's no longer adequate to say you will transplant your European and US success, even if it is a $3 billion to $4 billion brand. Marketing needs insights.

McEachern is now CEO of Strategic Solutions Group-Asia, a Hong Kong-based consultancy that he founded to advise companies on market entries, consumer brand building, CSR, and leadership development.

He is also an Adjunct Professor in the MBA and Executive MBA programs at HKUST, where he teaches about building powerful consumer brands in China, the fastest growing and most competitive consumer market in the world.

McEachern is also a founding board member of the PepsiCo Service Corps, an organization of senior executive retirees from the company who work with the PepsiCo Foundation to advance CSR projects on nutrition, health and wellness, and access to water.

* * *

Stephen S. Roach
Chairman, Morgan Stanley Asia

Stephen S. Roach

Stephen Roach is an internationally respected economist. Before becoming Chairman of Morgan Stanley Asia in April 2007, he was Morgan Stanley's Chief Economist, heading the company's global team of economists and became one of Wall Street's most influential thought leaders. He has long advised governments and policy makers around the world, and frequently presents expert testimony to the US Congress.

Roach's recent research has focused on globalization, the emergence of China and India, and the capital market implications of global imbalances. He is widely quoted in the financial press and other media and was bearish on the US market for years before the credit crisis in 2008.

"What we are going through now is not the end of the world, it's a cycle," he said in a lecture at HKUST in early 2009.

> What are some of the key issues to focus on for the next cycle? To me, that's what's at the core of the globalization debated. Do we stay with it, or do we backtrack to localization?

I admit I have been something close to a perennial bear on the US, but most of what I said has come to pass. I am not embarrassed to have been negative on the US. Over that time I have also been steadfast in my optimism with respect to Asia, especially China and India, not Japan, but many of the smaller countries as well, such as Korea and Taiwan.

I hope what they will call me at the end of the day is not the perennial bear or even the perennial Asian optimist, but just a realist.

Roach holds a PhD in Economics from New York University. Before joining Morgan Stanley in 1982, he was Vice President of Economic Analysis for the Morgan Guaranty Trust Company, served in a senior capacity on the research staff of the Federal Reserve Board in Washington DC, and was a research fellow at the Brookings Institution.

✳ ✳ ✳

James E. Thompson
Chairman, Crown Worldwide Holdings Ltd.

James Thompson, Chairman and CEO of Crown Group, has been based in Asia for more than 40 years. He set up his first removal company in Japan in 1965 with personal savings of just $500, and today oversees the largest privately owned international removal firm, with 200 locations in 50 countries.

James E. Thompson

The journey has been a long and sometimes bumpy one. Thompson linked up with an equal-equity joint partner in 1970, who left the company in 1978. Thompson bought him out, and moved his headquarters to Hong Kong.

Two years later, just as Crown was turning the corner after making the buyout payments, his chief financial officer set up a rival firm in early 1980, taking half the staff with him. "It was an absolutely major blow to me … you couldn't even trust the people closest to you. I almost wanted to quit the business," Thompson said.

Needless to say, he held out, and built Crown into a truly global enterprise. The company is a major player in international mobility management, relocation, records management, and logistics. It makes much use of IT to generate business and serve its clients, and in 2007 revenues reached $250 million.

> We are getting at least 10,000 quotation requests a year from individuals all over the world. They just type it into the Web. We have learned how to maximize the success of something like that—once you get that opportunity you jump all over it.

> We have our own significant IT team and with major clients we go to them and say, we will establish a website for you if we get your contract. It's a closed website that allows all of their staff to go in there, put in their details, and we follow it through. It's a big selling point, which you can do on a global basis. The corporate side gets all the statistical information they need, the customer gets the service they need.

Thompson has a Bachelor of Science degree in Aeronautical Engineering from San Jose State University, and was awarded the Gold Bauhinia Star by the Hong Kong government in 2003.

* * *

Marjorie Mun Tak Yang
Chair, Esquel Group

Marjorie Mun Tak Yang

Marjorie Yang is Chair of Esquel Group, a vertically integrated textile and apparel manufacturer, with operations stretching from cotton farming to accessories production to retail. The company emphasizes quality control, and clients include such firms as Abercrombie & Fitch, Tommy Hilfiger, Brooks Brothers, and Polo Ralph Lauren.

In its early days, however, Esquel traded in low-end products. It was founded in 1978 by Yang's father. Yang herself had been working in the US in investment banking, and was asked to return to Hong Kong to help run the new family firm.

When Yang became Chair of Esquel in 1995, she made it her mission to move the company upmarket and make "quality" its watchword. They already had good quality control over the production processes at their base in Gaoming in Guangdong province, where, over the years, more than $500 million has been invested in mills, factories, offices, dormitories, and facilities for workers.

She extended that control further by creating a vertical supply chain and acquiring cotton farms in Xinjiang to ensure a steady supply of high-quality cotton.

Yang also strengthened the company's focus on CSR, unveiling a related mission statement and five-point "eCulture" in 2003 to reinforce that commitment. The five points are ethics, the environment, exploration, excellence, and education.

> The garment industry has not really been an employer of choice in the past. It's not really cultivated that feel-good factor. My father was a very generous man, and he paid very well. We are trying to enhance that, to look at how we, as part of the garment business, can make people feel good.
>
> One thing you have to have is a unifying culture. We promote the Esquel culture to eliminate other differences and strengthen the corporate culture. We try to have a shared set of values so everybody from Vietnam to Seattle to Xinjiang can feel part of the group.

She has backed her commitment to CSR with investments in environmental controls in her factories and education and HIV/AIDs programs in Xinjiang and Gaoming.

Yang is also a member of the National Committee of the Chinese People's Political Consultative Conference. She earned a Bachelor of Science in Pure Mathematics from the Massachusetts Institute of Technology and an MBA from Harvard.

Note

1 See *Time*, "60 Years of Asian Heroes," 2006. http://www.time.com/time/asia/ 2006/heroes/bl_fung.html.

From Socialized Institution to Privatized Corporation

The Link Real Estate Investment Trust Experience (A case study)

Prepared by Isabella Chong

Under the supervision of Professor Steven J. DeKrey, Senior Associate Dean, Hong Kong University of Science and Technology

"Hey Paul, did you read the news about the major political groups urging the government to buy back shares of the Link REIT in the newspaper today? If only they listened to you and retained a certain degree of control, we would not have all these protests from the tenants!" Recalling his golf buddy's small talk, Paul Cheng, ex-chair of The Link Management Limited couldn't help but let out a sigh. Since his decision to relinquish the post of chair of Link Management Limited more than two years ago, he has been wondering now and then if, in the interests of the public, he should have brought the disagreement between him and the aggressive significant unit holder into the open and fought it out. His mind drifted back to how it all started with the government back in 2005, and how he tried to balance the interests of all stakeholders; investors, tenants, nearby residents and government.

In pursuing its investment strategy, the Manager will
- maintain a large and geographically diversified portfolio of:
  - convenience-based retail properties primarily serving the basic consumer needs of the residents of the Adjacent Housing Estates and other visitors[1]

Dogged by controversy, the world's largest real estate investment trust[2] and Hong Kong's first, The Link Real Estate Investment Trust (REIT; The Link), finally began trading on the Hong Kong stockmarket on November 25, 2005.

While the board cheered the more than 15 percent climb in its share price on its first trading day, it was also greeted with a protest mounted by activists and public housing residents outside the stock exchange, demanding the company continue charging the lowest rents at the properties.[3] The protestors were afraid that with the privatization of the malls and car parks, The Link would exploit the full commercial value of these properties, depriving the residents of suitable facilities made possible by the concessionary rental charges borne out of the Hong Kong Housing Authority's stated social conscience.

Since then, there has been a series of run-ins between the tenants and The Link management over rental increases. Activist groups have urged the government to intervene and certain legislators attempted to influence the management of The Link, but failed.[4]

To aggravate the matter further, within a few days of listing, The Children's Investment Management (TCI), a British hedge fund, bought 18.35 percent[5] of The Link's shares and became the largest shareholder. Seeking to reap profits quickly, their views did not exactly tie in with the Link executives and Cheng, the chair appointed by the government to balance the interests of public housing tenants and the Link's shareholders.[6] Cheng's strategy was to pace upgrading of assets and rent increases to give tenants time to adjust.

Refusing to adopt TCI's aggressive stand, Cheng announced his resignation in January 2007. After his departure, under leadership of the new chair and new senior management, asset improvement and rent increases sped up, prompting more protests from tenants. During the latest protest staged by the tenants of one of the indoor markets, one shopkeeper complained of a 360 percent increase in rent. When a legislator asked the government to urge The Link's management to help small tenants, the Secretary for Commerce and Economic Development said "the management had the right to determine its business strategy and operate in accordance with market principles."[7]

Indeed, The Link is a private company, and its only responsibility is to provide a return to shareholders and to abide by the law. This continued saga leads Cheng to wonder whether the Hong Kong Housing Authority (HA) should have listened to his suggestion and kept certain control over The Link. He couldn't help but ponder the difference between social responsibility and corporate responsibility, and whether divestment of similar assets in the future could be done in a more optimal way.

The Hong Kong Housing Authority

The HA is a statutory body established in 1973 under the Housing Ordinance, with origins dating back to the great fire of 1953, which wiped out the homes of some 50,000 people at the Shek Kip Mei squatter area.[8] This tragedy forced the Hong Kong government to break from its tradition of nonintervention to enter into the housing market. With a tight public purse and influx of refugees from China, progress was slow in the early years.

When Sir Murray MacLehose took over governorship of Hong Kong in late 1971 he was appalled by the inadequate and harsh living conditions of much of the population. With much more money in the public purse than his predecessors, the new governor set out an ambitious 10-year housing program, and the HA was formed with a mission to meet the housing needs of people who could not afford private housing.[9] Over the years, as Hong Kong became more affluent, the scale and scope of involvement grew relentlessly. The government evolved from building basic boxes for accommodation to developing modern self-contained communities, which include commercial, recreational, educational, welfare, and transport facilities.

Before the divestment in 2005, HA managed more than 10 percent of Hong Kong's retail space, and was the planner, designer, and developer, as well as operator of everything from homes for the elderly to shopping arcades and car parks. As of 2008, approximately one-third of Hong Kong's population was living in public rental housing units.[10]

Operating within the bureaucratic framework of the public sector, HA has often been influenced by public policy and socio-economic considerations. The properties were usually leased out at below market rates to small retailers. The agency has been operating at a deficit each year, and was expected to run into imminent financial crisis. In search of greater efficiency and prompted by a desire to move from the role of provider to facilitator, the HA looked for greater private sector involvement. Unlike the early days, there were no credible private-sector management firms. To explore the possibilities, in July 2002, the HA commissioned a consultancy project to investigate the feasibility and means of divesting its retail and car parking facilities. As a result, in 2003 the HA approved a plan to divest these assets. Although the decision was prompted by the need for greater efficiency and to address its serious financial problem, it was in line with the government's commitment to "free market" and "small government."[11] The exercise would also enable the HA to focus on its core business of providing subsidized public rental housing to people in need.

While the proceeds from the divestment would be used to cover the deficits, Michael Suen, Chair of the HA, believed the plan would provide a win–win situation.

> Commercial and domestic tenants are likely to benefit from the change to private ownership and management of the retail and car-parking facilities, as it will bring about enhanced quality, improved services and faster response to customer demand.[12]

The portfolio

A total of 180 facilities, comprising 149 integrated retail and car park facilities, two standalone retail facilities, and 29 standalone car park facilities were selected for the divestment. This portfolio of approximately 10.3 million square feet of retail space and 79,000

Figure A2.1: Retail facilities by internal floor area

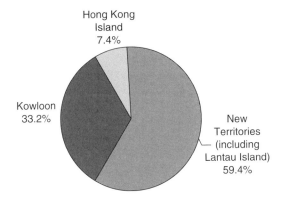

Source: Global Offering Circular, p. 3–4.

car parks is all located within government housing estates. These properties constitute roughly 9.1 percent of Hong Kong's total retail space and 13.7 percent of Hong Kong's total commercial car park spaces. They serve the daily needs of approximately 40 percent of Hong Kong's population who live in the adjacent public housing estates (see figures A2.1 and A2.2).

Figure A2.2: Car park facilities by number of car park spaces

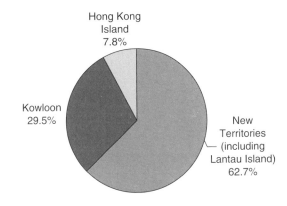

Source: Global Offering Circular, p. 3–4.

The first attempt

After more than 12 months of structuring and preparation work, The Link public offering was set to go on November 25, 2004. The government was expected to reap up to HK$32 billion through the listing.

However, the plan was derailed by two pensioners, who believed that the divestment of the malls and the car parking spaces would deprive them of "suitable facilities," which they enjoyed under the ownership of the HA.[13] They were concerned that privatization would lead to higher rental, which could result in an increase in the prices of merchandise sold. With support from certain legislators, they applied for a judicial review on December 8, 2004, claiming that the HA was breaching the housing code in selling the assets.[14]

Aside from "undermining the livelihood of the residents," with only 10 percent of The Link allotted for public float,[15] the government was also criticized for selling Hong Kong out to foreign interests as the strategic investor, CapitaLand Limited, and most of the nine cornerstone investors were foreign owned.

The case quickly became politicized and a media sensation.

Although the Court of First Instance and the Court of Appeal both ruled in favor of the HA, the legal proceedings got in the way of the original schedule. The listing scheduled for December 2004 had to be scrapped because the pensioners moved the case to the Final Court of Appeal. A final judgment upholding the earlier rulings was eventually handed down on July 20, 2005. Three months later the government announced its decision to relaunch The Link.

The Link

Reacting to opinion from certain sectors in society, which was greatly sensationalized by the media during the first listing attempt, the government cut out the nine cornerstone investors in favor of local small investors as a public relations initiative: Hong Kong assets for Hong Kong people. Initially, 30 percent of the units under the second global offering were allotted to Hong Kong small investors. Because the offer was 18 times oversubscribed, additional units amounting to another 9.9 percent of the HA's total unit entitlement under consideration for sale, were allocated to the public. In the end, about 40 percent of the total units sold went to local public investors.[16] A 5 percent discount was given on all Hong Kong Public Offering units. The Link IPO, the largest REIT in the world, was successfully executed on November 25, 2005. Net proceeds received by the HA from the divestment amounted to HK$33.8 billion.[17]

The Link REIT structure

Upon completion of the global offering, The Link became the beneficial owner of all the properties with management responsibilities vested in The Link Management Limited (the manager), an entity incorporated in February 2004 and a wholly owned subsidiary of the HA before the divestment (see figure A2.3). The manager's role was defined as

> to manage The Link REIT in accordance with the Trust Deed and, in particular to ensure that the financial and economic aspects of The Link REIT's assets are professionally managed in the sole interests of the Unitholders.[18]

The trustee, HSBC Institutional Trust Services (Asia) Limited, holds the shares of the manager on trust for the benefit of unitholders.

To ensure that the manager has the necessary experience and skills required for the task, CapitaLand Limited, one of the largest property companies in Asia, was engaged by the manager as a strategic partner. With support from CapitaLand, the manager is responsible for The Link's investment and financial strategies, asset improvement, acquisition, and disposal policies, and overall management of the properties. To align the interests of CapitaLand with those of The Link, CapitaLand invested $120 million worth of units at the time of the global offering as part of the terms of the agreement.

The manager

Since March 2005, the manager has been managing the portfolio under the direction of the HA and in line with the HA's policies.

Figure A2.3: The Link Management Limited—organizational structure

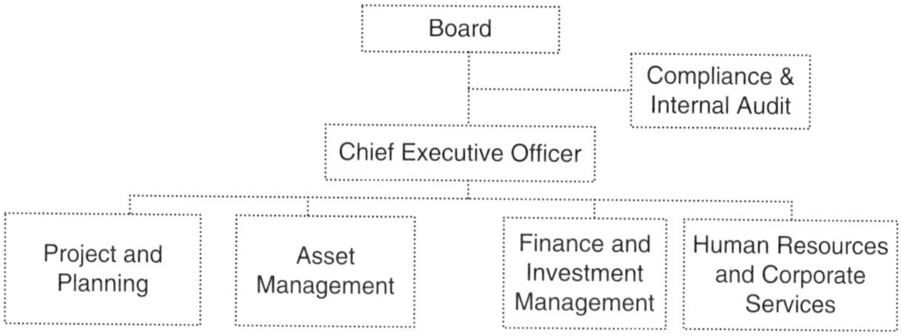

Source: Global Offering Circular, p.161.

Subsequent to the divestment, it operates within the framework established by the board.

Although the government did not retain any equity interest in The Link after the IPO, the HA put into place certain corporate governance policies to ensure that the manager would operate in a way that serves the interests of the unitholders as a whole and not the specific interests of a few.

To balance the interests of the public housing tenants and The Link's shareholders, Paul Cheng Ming-fun was appointed chair and Victor So Hing-woh the CEO by the HA.

Formerly chair of Inchcape Pacific Limited, Cheng has been active both as a corporate leader and in politics. He was a member of the Hong Kong Legislative Council before the handover and also served on the Provisional Legislature after 1997. So, on the other hand, was formerly executive director and the CEO of the Hong Kong Housing Society, an NGO and the second-largest public housing provider after the HA. Before joining the manager he was executive director of Sun Hung Kai Properties Limited.

At the time of divestment, about 25 percent of the staff at The Link management were previously employees of the HA.

Objective, guidelines, and strategy

> ...key objective...is to provide Unitholders with stable distributions per Unit with...sustainable long-term growth of such

distributions ... accomplish this objective through optimizing the performance and enhancing the overall quality ... of assets. ...[19]

To help achieve the objective of providing the unitholders with a stable, sustainable return, a set of investment guidelines was stated in the offering circular:

- invest in properties for the long-term;
- focus on sustainable income-producing properties with potential for long-term income and capital growth; and
- maintain a large and geographically diversified portfolio of:
  - convenience-based retail properties primarily serving the basic consumer needs of the residents of the Adjacent Housing Estates and other visitors; and
  - carparks serving the tenants and customers of the retail properties, the residents of the surrounding neighborhoods and other visitors.[20]

Both the trustee and the manager were required by the listing agreement to adhere to the investment policy for three years. Governed by the REIT Code in Hong Kong, the manager is required to distribute at least 90 percent of its audited net income afterward. At the time of listing, the yield to unitholders was forecasted to be about 5.53 percent on a listing price of HK$10.30 per unit.

Other key strategies included an active management style, expansion of the portfolio through selective acquisition, and improvement of financial management expertise. Furthermore, to ensure that a prudent capital structure is maintained, gearing ratio was capped at 45 percent.

Operating within these guidelines, bearing in mind the interests of unitholders and the livelihood of tenants, under Cheng and So the manager adopted a strategy of gradual improvement of assets to improve income. Cheng's plan was to pace asset improvement so that the tenants would have time to adjust not just to the new environment but also higher rent. He hoped that with improved accessibility and supporting facilities, more traffic would be attracted to the malls, and income for the tenants would improve over time.

> [Income from] the shops enabled many of the operators to put their children through school, we can't just raise the rent drastically within a short time span.[21]

Pressure from the public

Nevertheless, even with restraint on the scale of rental increases, such an exercise faced and continues to face strong resistance from tenants who were used to submarket rent. At the time of divestment, the HA was charging HK$12 per square foot at some of its malls while neighboring malls were renting at HK$40–50 per square foot.

Rental increases were greeted with protests and media coverage. Activists, speaking for all concerned parties, wanted the manager to charge the lowest rent at the malls and lowest parking fee at the car parks, and demanded fair market pay for cleaners, security guards, and other staff hired by its contractors. A civic organization, Linkwatch, comprising workers, activists, tenants, and academics, was created to keep watch over the manager's operations.[22] Certain legislators saw this as an opportunity to win favors and be champions for the "grass roots,", and called for the involvement of the Legislative Council (LegCo).[23] Cheng refused to appear in front of the LegCo to "explain" the management of the malls and car parks, and opinions were divided, with some questioning the wisdom and legitimacy of the LegCo's attempt to interfere with the operations of a private company.[24]

Pressure from a significant unitholder

While Cheng was busy defending the manager's rights and obligations in securing a reasonable return for its investors, he was at the same time under pressure from a significant unitholder, who emerged after three days of listing, to improve the return to unitholders at a faster pace.

With no cornerstone investors and a 40 percent allocation to retail investors, fund managers had to buy from the market to invest in The Link. The demand quickly pushed up the price of the units. Within three days of listing, it went from a subscription price of HK$10.30 to close at HK$12.25. Taking into consideration the 5 percent retail investor discount, the investment went up 25 percent in value in a very short period of time. As a result, many small investors took a profit. Thus, within a few days TCI was able to buy up to 18.35 percent of The Link REIT units from the market, and became a major shareholder of The Link.

TCI, one of the world's most successful funds, has a reputation for interfering with the corporate strategy of companies in which it has a stake, to reap profits quickly.[25] Its goal, therefore, was in conflict with Cheng's vision of balancing the interests of public housing tenants and The Link's unitholders.

The appointment of John Ho, head of the TCI office in Hong Kong in July 2006, to the board as a nonexecutive director put pressure on for quick rate increases and an aggressive rental policy. Cheng was said to have repeatedly ignored the hedge fund's requests for a more aggressive investment strategy and eventually stepped down as chair, on March 30, 2007, one year before the expiry of his contract. At the time of the announcement, a spokesman for The Link REIT said Cheng confirmed there was no disagreement with the board, but Cheng later admitted the rent-rise row forced him to resign.

> My resignation was the result of a clash between shareholder's interests and social responsibility... Many of these retailers are small businesses operating to earn money for their children's education.[26]

New era: changes in top management

After Cheng's resignation, the board appointed Nicholas Robert Sallnow-Smith as the new chair. Before joining Link Management Limited, Sallnow-Smith, a veteran of Hong Kong's property industry and 10 years Cheng's junior, was the CEO of Hongkong Land Limited, a leading property company with more than five million square feet of prime office and shopping space in the Central district of Hong Kong. He was appointed by Standard Chartered Bank three months later to be its Regional Chief Executive (North East Asia), and has held the position up to the time of writing.

Shortly after Cheng's resignation, Victor So, The Link's chief executive, also announced that he would not renew his contract upon its expiry in July 2007. Although he remained until November after his successor was found, the speculation was similar to that surrounding Cheng's departure—that So left because "the company's management found him not aggressive enough in improving The Link's performance."[27] Nevertheless, Sallnow-Smith stressed that there was no pressure to remove So.

Replacing So as the executive director and CEO was Ian David Murray Robins, the then Divisional Director and Head of Asia for Macquarie Real Estate Asia Limited. While So was Hong Kong educated and had worked in the public and private sector, as well as NGOs, in Hong Kong, Robins was educated in South Australia and spent most of his 20 years of working life in Australia and other parts of Asia.

Seven months later, in May 2008, two more executives were brought in from Macquarie Countrywide Trust in Australia, the sister company of Macquarie Real Estate Asia, to be the chief operating officer and the director of strategy. Although Macquarie Countrywide, a Sydney-based listed property trust that manages community-based retail facilities, has an asset value that is similar to that of The Link, the media questioned whether that experience would be applicable to managing low end shopping malls that serve the needs of residents at government housing estates.[28]

Direction

Mission Statement

To build The Link as a market-driven and value-creating asset manager offering—

- inviting shopping experiences to customers;
- prosperous business opportunities to tenants; and
- rewarding financial returns to investors.[29]

Asset improvement

With the new executives and new board, asset improvement became frenetic, to fulfill the mission statement that first appeared in the 2007 annual report. Eleven new projects were announced in 2007, bringing the total number of asset improvement projects to 26. As of March 2008, five had been completed, one had been deferred, and 20 were in progress, with two scheduled to start in 2009. With improved facilities, an upgraded physical structure, and promotional activities, the manager hoped to attract more shoppers to the malls. The trade mix of tenants has also been closely monitored and refined. Specialty shops and food and beverage outlets have been introduced despite the accusation by some that there has been a trend in favoring popular chain stores. These exercises were all geared toward improving the asset value of the properties and providing higher returns in the form of increases in traffic flow and rent.

Corporate citizenship

Other than upgrading the properties, the manager has also been active in launching seminars that help tenants, and activities that build community relationships.

For the tenants, they included the following:

- *Information and skills upgrade:* Since 2007, the manager has been organizing seminars for its tenants on such topics as security, management concepts, industry trends, retail techniques, and customer servicing. These seminars also served as sharing platforms. According to the 2008 annual report, more than 600 participants took part in these seminars. As a result of positive feedback, the Link Tenant Academy was formally launched in 2008.
- *Renovation and designs made easy:* Another service provided by the manager is the establishment of The Link Tenant Information Center. With the renovation and improvement of the shopping malls, many existing tenants have had to change their shop design in keeping with the new environment. The Link Tenant Information Center offers one-stop access to information on shop designs and products, to assist tenants in starting new outlets or renovating existing shops.

For the community, they included the following:

- *Workshops and activities:* In addition to providing nearby residents with a convenient shopping environment, the manager also uses the malls as community activity centers. The Link Fun Academy was established during the second half of 2007 to organize various workshops and activities for the public, such as calligraphy classes, an acting workshop for children, a musical training workshop, a youth soccer scheme, and parenting talks.

Since its inception, The Link Fun Academy has organized more than 40 activities, attracting about 8,000 participants. The aim is to create a cohesive and harmonious neighborhood.

As a service to the community, the manager has set aside 930,410 square feet, or 8.5 percent of the total lettable internal floor area,[30] to rent to nonprofit-making organizations at a concessionary rate. The Link has also sponsored venues for community organizations that carry out fundraising, civic education, and health and environmental protection education activities.

Reaction and feedback

The manager was named a "Caring Company" by the Hong Kong Council of Social Services in February 2008 for its contribution to and support of community activities. It was also awarded a Prime Award for Corporate Social Responsibility by the Prime Communications Limited and the Hong Kong Institute of Directors on October 31, 2008.[31] Among other judging criteria, it scored high marks for its readiness to take up CSR and show concern for social needs.

Shoppers

The results of three independent surveys conducted by organizations commissioned by the manager in 2006 and 2007 showed that customers' overall ratings of the shopping malls increased markedly after asset improvement, from 4.7 to 7.8 and 4.4 to 7.2. The survey, conducted in June 2006, also revealed that shoppers increased their visits after the mall had completed its improvement work.

The asset improvement projects, coupled with various activities organized by the management, seemed to succeed in attracting more visitors to the malls.

> Running a restaurant requires a good understanding of customers' tastes and market trends. Since reopening with a new look ... more popular ... also attracted many from outside our neighborhood ...[32]

> During weekends, we like having family time at shopping centers. We joined this promotional activity as a family unit and are very excited...[33]

Tenants

With asset improvement came rental increases. Some saw the development as positive, because some existing tenants were able to upgrade and new tenants signed up.

> We took the opportunity to renovate our shop in parallel... The shop front has now been given a much trendier outlook...to attract more customers and upgrade hand in hand with the shopping center....
>
> We believe in the new business approach and have therefore extended the branch network to The Link's shopping center for the first time. The result is surprisingly good...[34]
>
> The cooked food stalls...have donned a refreshing look and enhanced environmental hygiene after renovation. Customers...have demonstrated their support of the positive changes with their patronage.[35]

However, others resisted and protested against each rental increase, and this continued to attract media coverage. Wet-market tenants, who occupied 11 percent of the total retail floor space at the time of listing, together with vendors selling traditional medicine, incense sticks and other nonmainstream goods, continued to challenge The Link's rental increases.

On August 21, 2008, 78 vendors in Choi Ming wet market closed their business to demand assurance from The Link management for a "reasonable rent increase." A vendor who operates two seafood stalls said:

> The rent has risen twice since the opening of the wet market in 2002. My initial rent was about HK$20,000. It is now about HK$30,000.[36]

October saw two more protests from different properties. One shopkeeper in Yu Chui Court indoor market complained of a hefty increase in rent:

> For one chicken shop, the rent was increased from HK$5,000 a month to HK$23,000 a month. How can this possibly be sustained?[37]

Yet another in Lok Fu Shopping Center protested against The Link REIT after it increased rents from HK$30 a square foot to HK$130.

Although the companies managing the malls for The Link management explained that the rental increases were simply bringing rents to market level, some tenants were not satisfied and continued to seek support from politicians. Sallnow-Smith's comment in a news briefing further reaffirmed the commercial pricing strategy the manager had adopted:

> Every rent . . . is a market rent, and it will be different with every tenant because the store is different, the location is different and the potential income is different.[38]

In response to the protests, the government tried to exert its influence. Rita Lau, the Secretary for Commerce and Economic Development, said on November 13 that the government had written to The Link management to relay the concerns of its tenants about rent increases and to appeal on behalf of small shop tenants.[39] So far there has been no reply. It seemed while some directors were arguing that the small-to-medium retailers, who form "the backbone of the malls and provide necessities for nearby residents," could not afford big rental increases, activist shareholders of The Link were attacking the manager for not acting in the interests of shareholders over low rents.[40]

With the financial meltdown, more pressure has been put on The Link to cut rents. On November 26, the HA announced that it would reduce the rent in their malls by 50 percent for two months, thus providing the 6,000 tenants there temporary relief during the economic downturn. Legislator Tommy Cheung told the media that he hoped this would put pressure on private mall owners, including The Link.

However, The Link management, though prepared to help tenants, held different views. A spokeswoman relayed that boosting consumer spending was the way to help tenants.[41] To this end, a

HK$10 million promotional program was launched to stimulate consumer spending at the malls.

Conclusion

Coming out of SARS, the HA was pressed to find financial resources so that it could continue to provide housing for those who could not afford private properties. Its divested assets were run-down, mostly in secondary and nonprime locations, and were inefficiently run. The rent charged was a fraction of the market price. The privatization of these assets enabled the HA to solve its financial crisis yet the new organization—The Link—inherited a group of tenants who were used to socialized rent.

In reaction to criticism from its first listing attempt, the HA gave up all of its unit entitlement to public investors, because of the overwhelming response from the public to the listing offer. This gave TCI, a UK-based hedge fund, an opportunity to come in and exert influence on management. Then-Chair Paul Cheng, with social responsibility in mind and in tune with the HA, disagreed and resigned, thus giving way to a team of foreign executives. The new management team under Sallnow-Smith and Robins has taken a more commercial stance. The company has been upgrading the assets and rent at a fast pace. The yield to investment has improved under the new management, yet protests have also become more frequent. Nevertheless, the management has also been doing its part in being a good corporate citizen, as seen from the various community services and projects it has initiated and undertaken. Some legislators still cling to the old operating mode, and hold The Link responsible for the livelihood of small tenants. So where does corporate responsibility end and social responsibility begin?

Notes

1 The Link Real Estate Investment Trust Global Offering Circular, November 2006, 59.
2 Fiona Lau, "Link Debut Gives Reason for Cheer: Retail Investors Enjoy 20pc Gain as the REIT's First Day Exceeds Expectations," *South China Morning Post*, November 26, 2005, 1.
3 *South China Morning Post*, "Listing Success Not the End to Link's Challenges," November 26, 2005, 16.

4 Andrew Work, "A Whipping Boy for Our Socialists," *South China Morning Post*, January 18, 2007, 14.

5 Foster Wong, "Link REIT Douses Talk TCI Seeks Change at the Top," *South China Morning Post*, August 24, 2006.

6 Albert Cheng, "Damage limitation," *South China Morning Post*, May 5, 2007.

7 Dennis Chong, "Shops shut in protest at rent rises imposed by The Link contractors," *South China Morning Post*, October 30, 2008, 2.

8 Tony Miller, "Public Sector Reform: The Housing Authority Example," February 22, 1999. www.housingauthority.gov.hk/en/print/0,1-100-2-0-2376,00.htm.

9 Murray MacLehose, "Social and Economic Challenges," in Sally Blyth & Ian Wotherspoon (eds.) *Hong Kong Remembers* (Hong Kong: Oxford University Press, 1996), 114–27.

10 Hong Kong Housing Authority n.d., www.housingauthority.gov.hk/en/aboutus/ha/0,00.htm.

11 Hong Kong Housing Authority n.d., www.housingauthority.gov.hk/en/print/0,1-96-2-0-6928,00.htm.

12 Ibid.

13 Jane Moir, "Pensioners' Attempt to Sink the Link May Cause a Few Sweaty Brows," *South China Morning Post*, December 11, 2004, 12.

14 Paul Cheng, "The Link REIT Case," Hong Kong University of Science and Technology, Presentation to Kellogg-HKUST Executive MBA Class, February 15, 2009.

15 Moir, op. cit.

16 Kenneth Mak, "Memorandum for the Housing Authority: Report on the Divestment Project," n.d., www.housingauthority.gov.hk/hdw/content/document/en/aboutus/ha/paperlibrary/ha/HA0106.

17 The Link Annual Report 2006, 24.

18 Global Offering Circular, 178.

19 Ibid., 59.

20 Ibid.

21 Paul Cheng, Interview with case writer, October 16, 2008.

22 Linkwatch website, www.linkwatch.hk.

23 Work, op. cit.

24 Jake Vanderkamp, "Sorry, Legislators, You Can't Have Your Link Cake and Eat It, Too," *South China Morning Post*, May 12, 2006.

25 James Mackintosh "TCI hedge fund loses more than $1bn in its worst month ever," *South China Morning Post*, July 15, 2008.

26 *South China Morning Post*, January 28, 2008.

27 Denise Hung and Danny Mok, "The Link to Lose CEO in Mid-July REIT Chief Executive to Step Down at End of contract 'for Health Reasons,'" *South China Morning Post*, May 1, 2007.

28 Ben Kowk "The Link REIT Takes a New Tack in Mall Management...," *South China Morning Post*, May 6, 2008.

29 The Link Annual Report 2007, 5.

30 As of September 30, 2008.

31 The Link Interim Report 2008/09, 14.

32 The Link Annual Report 2008, 35.

33 Ibid., 38.

34 The Link Annual Report 2007, 47.

35 The Link Annual Report 2008, 37.

36 *South China Morning Post*, August 21, 2008.

37 *South China Morning Post*, October 30, 2008.

38 *South China Morning Post*, November 13, 2008.

39 Fulton Mak "Despite Concerns, The Link Sidesteps Calls to Cut Rents," *South China Morning Post*, November 13, 2008.

40 Ibid.

41 Fox Yi Hu "Housing Authority to halve rent at 6,000 shops for two months," *South China Morning Post*, November 26, 2008.

Index